JUN 1 4 2004

Tiffin Glass 1940-1980:

Figurals, Paperweights, Pressed Ware

Ruth Hemminger, Ed Goshe and Leslie Piña

with a preface by John Bing

4880 Lower Valley Road, Atglen, PA 19310 USA

Library of Congress Cataloging-in-Publication Data

Hemmiinger, Ruth.
Tiffin glass 1940-1980 : figurals, papeweights, pressed ware / Ruth Hemminger, Ed Goshe, and Leslie Piña.
p. cm.
ISBN 0-7643-1422-X
1. Tiffin Glass Company--Catalogs. 2. Glassware--Collectors and collecting--Ohio--Tiffin--Catalogs. I. Goshe,
Ed. II. Piña, Leslie A., 1947-III. Title.
NK5198.T53 A4 2001
748.29171'24--dc21
2001001211

Designed by Leslie Piña
Layout by Bonnie M. Hensley
Type set in Korinna BT

ISBN: 0-7643-1422-X
Printed in China
1 2 3 4

Published by Schiffer Publishing Ltd.
4880 Lower Valley Road
Atglen, PA 19310
Phone: (610) 593-1777; Fax: (610) 593-2002
E-mail: Schifferbk@aol.com
Please visit our web site catalog at **www.schifferbooks.com**

In Europe, Schiffer books are distributed by Bushwood Books
6 Marksbury Avenue Kew Gardens
Surrey TW9 4JF England
Phone: 44 (0) 20-8392-8585; Fax: 44 (0) 20-8392-9876
E-mail: Bushwd@aol.com
Free postage in the UK. Europe: air mail at cost.

This book may be purchased from the publisher.
Include $3.95 for shipping. Please try your bookstore first.
We are always looking for people to write books on new and related subjects.
If you have an idea for a book please contact us at the Atglen, PA. address.
You may write for a free catalog.

Contents

Acknowledgments

This volume documents many of the pressed patterns, paperweights and figurals that were produced by the Tiffin Glass Company from 1940 to 1980. We would like to acknowledge and thank the following people who loaned glassware or furnished information to help make this book as comprehensive as possible: Carol J. Chaney, Eunice I. Cover, Robert and Donna Overholt, The Gallery – Richard and Beverly Digby, Dee and Tony Mondloch, Richard and Virginia Distel, Jean M. Eachus, Mr. and Mrs. Michael A. Wagner, Paul J. Williams, Gene and Jodi Haugh, Gary C. and Jan L. Dundore, Rosalie Adams, Howard and Janet Beisner, Michael Carlson, Harold and Betty Scherger, Ann Forrest, Michael A. Bridinger, Dawn Keough, Phil and Rayella Engle, Robert and Anne Jones, Kelly O'Kane, Jon and Linda Eakin, Paul and Nellie Haugh, Russ Gangloff, Carol and Larry Shook, Madolyn Key, Brian Courtney, Geralyn Lang, the Seneca County Museum, and the Tiffin Glass Museum.

We are also grateful to John Bing for his assistance with the manuscript and Lyman Hemminger and Ramon Piña for their hours of help with the photo sessions.

Preface

by John Bing

For many years I have enjoyed knowing members of the Tiffin Glass Collectors Club. What a fine group of people. They share a passion for glass and are that special breed of folk for whom collecting is a joy and a solace. Perhaps we are all collectors at heart. To hunt, to search, to gather, and to bring home are fundamental human activities. But what we choose to collect may make a great deal of difference. I believe there is a relationship between what a man or woman collects and what kind of person they become. I believe there is a reason why glass collectors, on the whole, are such a wonderful group of people.

Art glass is an object both of beauty and of craft. As a standard of craft, its study and its possession demonstrate again and again the skill and ingenuity, the care and the precision of its makers. To hold and to carefully consider that which is well made cannot help but have an effect on a life. We become that which we respect. We evaluate our own efforts by such models. In learning to discriminate between objects of exceptional craft, we establish high goals for ourselves. We measure our work and ourselves by these high standards. And given that these craftsmen were our forebearers, their message is all the more meaningful. Their work is part of our direct inheritance. We honor that work not only by collecting their craft, but also by maintaining their tradition of fine workmanship in our own lives.

And as a work of great beauty, art glass also contributes to the quality of our lives. Can one surround oneself with beauty and not be changed? True quality seems to grow like a seed in a life. It crowds out lesser works; it welcomes its equals. Matched against it, the cheap, the obvious, the cleverly commercial loses appeal and place.

One can be a collector of many things. For those who collect glass, and especially glass of the quality of Tiffin, there are true rewards, and some are only gradually realized as the nature of the collection slowly changes the life of the collector.

Introduction

The Tiffin Glass Company produced a wide variety of products, many of which have not been previously documented. This book presents an attempt to document the pressed ware, paperweights, and figurals that were produced at the Tiffin and Glassport factories from 1940-1980. Due to space constraints, it is impossible to include an example of every item in these categories. All of the colors that were produced during this time period are included.

The Color Guide illustrates the colors that Tiffin used from 1940-1980 for its pressed ware, but the reader should note that colors in the Guide will sometimes vary from the true color of the glass. In addition to the difficulties involved with providing accurate photographs of the glass, such variations can be attributed to the thickness of the glass, the length of refiring time, or batch variances. The Color Guide can also help to identify a piece of Tiffin Glass, especially when the glass shape is unknown. However, collectors must remember that other companies' colors will also resemble Tiffin's.

Company terminology is used in the captions to describe items, with object and color names capitalized. The dimensions are measured at the widest point. An "h" indicates that the height is the largest dimension of the object. Line numbers and production dates are taken from company catalogs and interoffice correspondence. Words or phrases within double quotation marks are the authors' terms used when documentation was lacking.

Prices are listed in U.S. dollars at the end of the caption. Each item is priced using a value range. These values were derived from actual purchase prices, from prices seen at antique shows or shops, internet online auctions, and an item's rarity and desirability. The prices are listed in the order in which the respective pieces appear in the photo. These values are intended as a guide, and neither the authors nor the publisher are responsible for any transactions based on this Guide.

c. 1915 photograph of the Tiffin Glass factory, located at the corner of 4th Avenue and Vine Street. Note the streetcar tracks running alongside the factory. The streetcar was the means of daily transportation for many of the glassworkers.

History of the Tiffin Glass Company

In July, 1888, it was announced that the A. J. Beatty & Sons glass factory of Steubenville, Ohio, would be relocating to Tiffin, Ohio. A. J. Beatty had been negotiating with various communities for more than a year to establish a site for the new factory. The city of Tiffin offered five years of natural gas, $35,000 in cash, and land valued at $15,000. Construction of a three-furnace glass factory at the corner of Fourth Avenue and Vine Street began in September, 1888, and operations commenced on August 15, 1889. Early production capacity was reported to be 500,000 pressed tumblers per week.

A. J. Beatty & Sons merged with the United States Glass Company on January 1, 1892, and became one of nineteen factories of the large corporation. The Tiffin factory was designated Factory R. On May 23, 1893, less than two years later, Factory R was destroyed by fire. The factory was rebuilt in Tiffin in return for two additional years of free natural gas.

Although Factory R started out as a pressed ware factory, after 1900 Factory R's main production was blown tableware. The Glassport factory, designated as Factory G, located near Pittsburgh, Pennsylvania, was incorporated in the United States Glass Company combine c. 1895. Throughout its history, Glassport's production focused primarily on pressed ware.

United States Glass Company products were marked with a gold-colored shield with the letters USG intertwined. After September 1927, household goods were identified by a gold paper label with TIFFIN superimposed over a large "T" within a shield. At this time, many of the items produced at Factory G, were marked with the Tiffin paper label, including the satinware, to capitalize on the prestige of the Tiffin name. Commercial ware continued to be marketed with the USG label.

While most of the factories within the United States Glass Company were forced to close during the Great Depression of the 1930s, Factory R and Factory G managed to survive. In June, 1938, the offices of the United States Glass Company were transferred from Pittsburgh to Tiffin with C. W. Carlson as President. By 1940, all glassware was marked with a Tiffin label; however, the official name of the company remained the United States Glass Company through 1962.

Although the focus of Tiffin's production continued to be stemware, a new line of modern designs contributed to the prosperity of the Tiffin factory. In 1938, Mr. Carlson introduced the Swedish Modern line, consisting of heavy offhand shapes. The Swedish Modern name was changed to Tiffin Modern in May 1946, to clarify that the glassware was American-made. Interest in Tiffin Modern free-form designs continued into the 1960s. At this time Glassport's production continued to be pressed tableware lines and commercial ware.

In 1955, the United States Glass Company purchased many of the molds and glass making equipment

August 24, 1940, Andy Joabson, Roy Willams, Joe Reese. Andy Joabson was head of the etching and decorating departments in the 1930s and 1940s; Roy Williams was head of the blowing department; Joe Reese was plant manager.

of the Duncan and Miller Glass Company, following the closing of their factory in Washington, Pennsylvania. A number of the Duncan and Miller glass workers relocated to Tiffin at that time. In 1956, a Duncan and Miller Division was created within the United States Glass Company, headed by James Duncan.

Many of the original Duncan and Miller lines were reproduced at both the Glassport and Tiffin factories, and marketed as Duncan and Miller. In addition, several old United States Glass Company pressed patterns were reissued and sold under the Duncan and Miller name, i.e.

Grape, Betsy Ross, and Williamsburg. This use of the Duncan and Miller label continues to be a source of confusion among Tiffin Glass collectors.

In 1958 serious financial difficulties arose within the corporation, resulting in the sale of the assets to a New York investment firm. Business conditions did not improve and a second sale took place in March, 1961 to Brilhart Plastics Corporation of Mineola, New York. In 1962 bankruptcy occurred; the Tiffin factory however, remained open until early 1963.

In 1963, four former employees—Paul Williams, C. W. Carlson Jr., Ellsworth Beebe, and Beatrice Platt—bought the plant and renamed it the Tiffin Art Glass Corporation. Incorporation took place May 1, 1963. The start-up date for the new venture was September 16, 1963. This transaction marked the end of the United States Glass Company. A great loss was incurred on August 3, 1963, when the Glassport factory was destroyed by a tornado. Nevertheless, business improved with $2,000,000 in annual sales.

On June 4, 1966, the company was sold again, this time to a major corporation, the Continental Can Company, in exchange for 6,462 shares of Continental common stock. The company was renamed the Tiffin Glass Company, Inc. During these years, stemware remained the major focus of production, with blown and pressed ware also manufactured.

The factory changed hands again when it was purchased in December, 1968, by another large corporation, Interpace, the parent company of Franciscan, Shenango, and Meyer China. It continued to be known as the Tiffin Glass Company; but, in addition to using the gold Tiffin shield, Interpace began to use a paper label, "Franciscan Crystal," which they placed on selected stemware lines in May 1969. This practice continued for two years.

On May 10, 1979, the factory was sold for the last time to Towle Silversmiths and operated as Tiffin Crystal, a division of Towle Silversmiths. The furnaces were shut down on May 1, 1980, the date considered by collectors to be the end of the Tiffin Glass Company. The Outlet Store and a decorating shop remained open until October, 1984, when the facility permanently closed. Towle later donated the factory and land to the city of Tiffin in exchange for a $1.1 million tax write-off. The city offered the property free to any company that would bring 100 jobs into the city. Unable to find a tenant, the city demolished part of the factory in late December, 1985, and January, 1986.

After production had ceased in 1980, the molds were dispersed and Russell Vogelsong of Summit Art Glass Company of Ravenna, Ohio, acquired the Tiffin shield trademark mold. The Tiffin Glass Collectors Club subsequently purchased this mold in 1991. To date, the logo has been reproduced by the Club in five colors: pink, cobalt blue, red, green, and purple, some with satin or iridized finishes.

In December, 1992 Maxwell Crystal of Tiffin, Ohio, was granted the registration of the Tiffin trademark. Gold Tiffin labels were placed on reproduction stemware lines, Christmas ornaments, and paperweights. In 1997, following legal action, Maxwell Crystal's right to the Tiffin trademark was revoked.

Over the years, Tiffin Glass products were identified by means of various paper labels. In 1969 a stylized Tiffin acid stamp was used to identify some stemware lines; this mark was used intermittently through the 1970s. Also during the 1970s some products were marked by the application of an acid stamp of the Tiffin shield trademark.

Today, twenty years after the furnaces were closed down, collectors continue to seek out Tiffin's beautiful stemware, decorative Modern art glass, pressed patterns, and hand-fashioned paperweights.

November 1954 photograph taken at a Toledo Engineering oyster party. Left to right: C.W. Carlson Jr., Clyde Dutton, Roy Williams, Bill Wolf, Ellsworth Beebe, and Jim O'Brien.

Above: Gov. James Rhodes, C.W. Carlson Jr., Paul Williams. Following the bankruptcy of the United States Glass Company in 1962, the Tiffin Glass factory resumed operations as the Tiffin Art Glass Corporation on September 16, 1963. Officers of the new corporation were: President, C.W. Carlson Jr., Vice President, Ellsworth Beebe (who passed away before operations resumed), Secretary/Plant Engineer, Paul Williams, and Treasurer, Beatrice Platt. The reopening of the Glass House was important not only to the unemployed glassworkers, but also to the city of Tiffin, with the creation of approximately 100 new jobs. Several officials from the State of Ohio were on hand to celebrate the factory's grand opening, including Governor James Rhodes and Senator Robin Turner. Also present was former United States Glass Company President C.W. Carlson Sr., who aided in the reestablishment of the Tiffin Glass operations.

Top right: Mid 1960s photograph showing administration of the Tiffin Art Glass Company. William Carlson, President; Dick Cook, Packaging/Sales; Paul Williams, Secretary and Plant Engineer.

Right: December 21, 1970 intracompany correspondence detailing how the various Franciscan Crystal labels were to be used.

1-1005

INTRACOMPANY CORRESPONDENCE

CORPORATION

DATE   Tiffin/December 21, 1970

TO

Joe Maxwell	Irene Betz
Don West	Mary Miller
Charles Feasel	Lottie Heck
Anita Nusbaum	Della Fowler
William Wolf	Betty Barlekamp

SUBJ: NEW PRODUCT LABELS

1) Franciscan Masterpiece Crystal with imprinted pattern names (with self-adhesive on printed surface/face down on backing) To be applied on all Franciscan "A" patterns stemware which include the Villeroy & Boch. Adhere on bottom of base to read through from above.

2) Franciscan Masterpiece Crystal (without pattern names) To be applied to Villeroy & Boch gift items; cut compotes, Palais Versailles accessories and all "B" pattern stemware.

3) Franciscan Crystal - Madeira To be applied only to the six shapes in the Madeira Crystal Casual Line/all colors.

4) Franciscan Crystal (without name) To be applied to all items other than above; i.e., Canterbury gifts, etc.

We should have all of the new labels on hand from the supplier and all regular-line items should be labeled with one of the four labels described above. If there are any questions, please let me know.

C. W. Carlson, Jr.

CWC:mz

cc: C. F. Assenheimer

Gold paper label with Tiffin, Hand Made, and the word Crystal at the bottom of the T. Not known when or how this sticker was used for certain. This sticker was found applied to a seafood cocktail, commonly produced in the 1950s.

Left: Gold Tiffin label used starting in September 1927 through c. 1950. Note the lack of the words "Hand Made."
Right: This sticker was used on stemware lines in the late 1960s, identifying the pattern name.

Left: Blue sticker used on stemware lines in the late 1970s, reading: "Hand Made Tiffin Crystal."
Right: Gold sticker used from c. 1950-1978. "Hand Made Tiffin."

Left: "Handmade by Duncan" label used on pressed ware lines from 1957-1962.
Center: "Franciscan Masterpiece Crystal," used during the Interpace years, 1970-1978.
Right: "Franciscan fine crystal, Interpace," seldom-seen silver foil label, probably used on the better-selling stemware lines after the Masterpiece Crystal promotion was discontinued.

United States Glass Company paper label. Commonly found on items from the 1920s and 1930s.

Blue sticker commonly found on Crystal or Milk Glass items which were produced at Glassport during the 1950s. Hand Made Tiffin.

Green Tiffin label. This sticker was used on some items produced in the last two years of the factory, 1979 and 1980.

Gold sticker used by Maxwell Crystal c. 1993-May, 1997. The label has an R in a circle registration mark.

Color Guide

The colors shown here include only the main production colors used for the pressed ware from 1940 to 1980.

Copen Blue. Introduced in the 1940s, Copen Blue was used for the production of pressed ware, c. 1958-1970.

Killarney. A dark green color, Killarney was introduced in 1948, and produced through about 1955.

Tiffin Rose. Tiffin Rose is often mistaken for the Wistaria color. Wistaria, introduced in the late 1940s, and produced through about 1955, is a vibrant pink color with reddish tones. The Tiffin Rose color is similar to Wistaria, but is paler in appearance. Tiffin Rose was produced in 1962 and 1963.

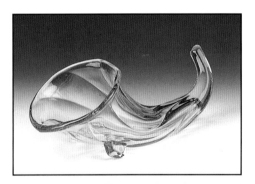

Dawn/Twilight. This lavender color produced c. 1951-1980, changes to a pale blue under fluorescent lighting.

Wild Rose. Wild Rose was used for both pressed and blown items, c. 1956.

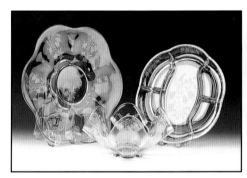

Crystal. Many of the pressed ware lines produced in Crystal from 1940 to 1980, were manufactured at both the Glassport and Tiffin factories.

Smoke. The Smoke color varies from shades of gray to brown, produced in the late 1950s, and then again in the 1970s.

Ruby. The Ruby color was used in the late 1950s and early 1960s for the Empress Line and the Pall Mall swans.

Persimmon. Produced in the early 1960s, Persimmon was used for blown and pressed pieces. Usually orange in appearance, the color varies from yellow to red-orange, sometimes with an opalescence.

Flame. Flame is very similar in appearance to the Amberina color from the 1920s and 1930s. The Flame color is usually found on the Murano, Tear Drop, and Canterbury lines.

Cobalt Blue. Cobalt Blue was used in the early 1940s for blown ware. In 1961 and 1962, a limited amount of pressed ware and blown ware was produced in this color.

Citron Green. Introduced c. 1964, Citron Green is a bright yellow-green. Citron Green is sometimes mistaken for Duncan and Miller's chartreuse color; however, chartreuse is slightly paler in appearance.

Empire Green. An emerald-green color, Empire Green was used in the manufacture of blown and pressed ware, introduced 1961. Produced for approximately one year, Empire Green is an extremely hard color to find.

Greenbriar. This avocado color was very popular, c. late 1960s through early 1970s.

Desert Red. A deep amber color with reddish tones, Desert Red was produced from c. 1965-1978.

Pine. A lighter shade of green than Killarney, Pine was produced c. 1952-1956.

Plum. Plum was introduced in 1961, and was used in the production of both blown and pressed ware. In the 1920s, this same shade was called Amethyst.

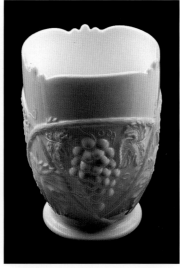

Milk Glass. Most of the Milk Glass production took place at the Glassport factory during the 1950s.

Golden Banana. A deep honey-gold color, Golden Banana was introduced in 1961, and was used for blown and pressed ware.

Black. Limited production of Black occurred in the late 1950s and again in the late 1970s. This opaque black color differed from the translucent black produced from c. 1925 to 1937.

11

Chapter 1

Tiffin Pressed Patterns

Pressed ware was an important part of Tiffin's production from 1940-1980. For the most part, the colored ware was made at Tiffin and the Crystal and Milk Glass items were produced at Glassport. The majority of the pressed ware patterns consisted of reissues of old United States Glass Company lines, and the Duncan and Miller molds which were purchased in 1955.

King's Crown

The King's Crown design is a line with a long history and numerous reproductions. This pattern was first made in about 1890 by Adams and Company of Pittsburgh, Pennsylvania, and was called X.L.C.R. or Excelsior. Production of X.L.C.R. continued when Adams and Company joined the United States Glass Company combine in 1891 and Adams then became known as Factory A. Most production was in Crystal and Crystal with ruby stain. The Crystal with ruby stain pieces remain favorites with collectors today. X.L.C.R. continued to be produced through at least 1904. The four bottle castor set was still listed in a 1926 United States Glass Company catalog, and a 1941 inventory included three X.L.C.R. items: a goblet, sundae and wine.

United States Glass Company reissued the X.L.C.R. pattern as Dubonnet in 1943. The same stemware molds appear to have been reused, but all the serving pieces were made from new molds. The Dubonnet pieces can be distinguished by the extra band of stain on the bottom of the stemware bowl, as well as on the rim. Dubonnet was produced with cranberry or ruby stain for about a two-year period.

The first appearance of a name change to King's Crown appears in a 1952 United States Glass Company price listing. King's Crown was being offered in Milk Glass, Crystal, and Crystal with cranberry or ruby stain, and was listed as #4016. The United States Glass Company also used the moniker Thumbprint and Old Thumbprint in advertising this design, but King's Crown is the name that is used by collectors today. In 1956, in addition to cranberry and ruby stain decoration, #121 Copper and Golden Nineties treatments were also offered. #121 Copper and Golden Nineties are not stain, but a paint that was applied to the rims. King's Crown with blue stain was offered from 1958 through 1962. In 1960, an allover gold decoration was available on the 7 3/8" plate and the stemware. Also in 1960, the King's Crown line started to be machine-pressed, in addition to being hand-pressed, the traditional method of production. The hand-pressed ware cost about 33% more than the machine-pressed ware.

Production of the Dubonnet and King's Crown blanks occurred at Glassport, while at least some, if not all, of the decorating was done at Tiffin. King's Crown was not listed in any company catalog after 1962.

1898 United States Glass Company catalog page featuring the X.L.C.R. pattern, later popularly known as the King's Crown design.

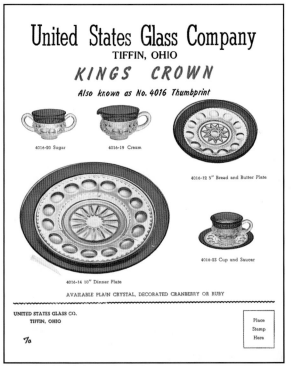

King's Crown catalog pages, c. 1957.

Reproductions abound for King's Crown. In interoffice correspondence dated 1959, United States Glass Company officers were lamenting the fact that Indiana Glass of Dunkirk, Indiana, had "copied" and "pirated" the King's Crown pattern produced by U.S. Glass. Indiana Glass introduced their Crown or "King's Crown" design in 1959, and have offered many colors and decorations over the years. Some of the solid colors produced by Indiana are milk glass, purple, yellow, amber, crystal, teal, and olive. Decorations include crystal with cranberry, ruby, yellow, or blue stain, and crystal with platinum or gold. The Tiffin and Indiana stems, at first glance, look nearly identical, but are rather easy to distinguish from one another. The Tiffin stems are made from a 3-part mold, and have nine thumbprints, while Indiana stems are made from a 2-part mold, and have eight thumbprints. The one exception is the sundae. Twelve thumbprints appear on both companies' stems, but the number of mold marks remain the same. The Indiana Glass serving pieces also differ from the Tiffin serving pieces. In addition to most of the shapes being different, the Tiffin pieces often have a "star" or "rayed" bottom, while the Indiana pieces do not have the "star."

The cups and saucers, and creams and sugars from the Indiana and Tiffin lines look alike, but they are also easy to distinguish from one another. Tiffin's cups, creams, and sugars are made from a 4-part mold, while Indiana's are produced from a 2-part mold. Indiana Glass "King's Crown" pieces are usually labeled with a Colony sticker, because Indiana is a division of Lancaster Colony Corporation, which is based in Columbus, Ohio. Indiana produced King's Crown in cobalt for Tiara Exclusives, which was also a division of Lancaster Colony during the 1980s and 1990s. In addition, Indiana produced items in ruby and green for the L.G. Wright Co.

The Indiana Glass "King's Crown" reproductions are quite plentiful in the secondary market, but other companies have reproduced the pattern as well. Glasscrafts and Ceramics, Inc. of Yonkers, New York, a wholesale distributor, offered six sizes of stems, 8 1/2" plate, and a finger bowl in crystal with ruby stain in 1953.

The Rainbow Art Company, located in Huntington, West Virginia, purchased blanks from U.S. Glass and decorated the ware at the Rainbow factory, c. 1945.

The L.G. Wright Co. of New Martinsville, West Virginia, offered numerous items in the 1960s, including: goblet, champagne, wine, cordial, sauce dish, covered compote, individual cream and sugar, 8" plate, sherbet, cup and saucer, cake stand, lemonade tumbler, small tumbler and two tall oil lamps. One of the oil lamps has a King's Crown base and a daisy and button font, and the other oil lamp has a King's Crown base with a milk glass beaded font. These items were offered in crystal with a pale ruby stain and amber stain, and in solid colors of ruby and green. Some of the crystal items have been seen with the Black Forest etching. This etching was originally applied to Paden City blanks.

In the 1930s, the D.C. Jenkins Glass Company of Kokomo, Indiana, offered a goblet, wine, and claret in crystal.

More reproductions were made in 1966 by the Imperial Glass Corporation, located in Bellaire, Ohio. Imperial produced a sherbert, cocktail, and a 8" h. candlestick in crystal with cranberry stain.

Nowadays, collectors look for King's Crown, often without regard to the original manufacturer. Stemware is readily available, and prices are modest. Many of the serving pieces, however, bring top dollar, due to their scarcity.

15 pc. Punch Set, with foot
Capacity 12 qts. Diameter 23"

15 pc. Punch Set Flared
Capacity 12 qts. Plate Diameter 23"

4016-39 Party Server 24" Diameter 8" High

Page 4   AVAILABLE PLAIN CRYSTAL, DECORATED CRANBERRY OR RUBY

4016-35 Wedding Bowl and Cover
6" Diameter 10½" High

4016-27 Flower Floater 12½" Diameter

4016-15 Torte Plate 14½" Diameter

4016-17 Ash Tray 5¼" Square

4016-32 Footed Cake Salver
12½" Diameter 4¾" High

AVAILABLE PLAIN CRYSTAL, DECORATED CRANBERRY, RUBY OR BLUE   Page 5

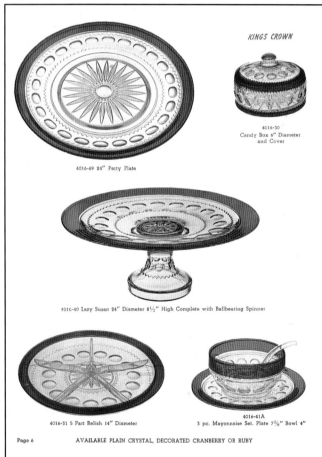

4016-30
Candy Box 6" Diameter
and Cover

4016-69 24" Party Plate

4016-40 Lazy Susan 24" Diameter 8½" High Complete with Ballbearing Spinner

4016-31 5 Part Relish 14" Diameter

4016-41A
3 pc. Mayonnaise Set. Plate 7⅜" Bowl 4"

Page 6   AVAILABLE PLAIN CRYSTAL, DECORATED CRANBERRY OR RUBY

4016-53 48 oz. Pitcher

4016-45 Ftd. Crimped Bowl

4016-48 Ftd. Flared Bowl

4016-42 Ftd. Salver

4016-63 Flat Compote

4016-47 Ftd. Crimped Compote

4016-66 2 Hld. Flared Nappy

4016-64 2 Hld. Crimped Bon Bon

4016-65 2 Hld. Plate

4016-67
2 Hld. 2-part May Bowl

4016-68
Small Crimped Compote

4016-50 Ftd.
Compote

4016-44 Ftd.
Candy Box and Cover

Page 7

King's Crown.

Above: July 1943 "China and Glass" advertisement for Dubonnet, which was later renamed King's Crown.

Left: King's Crown.

Below: Assortment of King's Crown items with various decorations.
Crystal with allover gold decoration #4016-1, 9 oz. Goblet, c. 1956. $20-25.
Milk Glass #4016-1, 9 oz. Goblet. $15-20.
Milk Glass #4016-5, 2 1/4 oz. Cocktail, c. 1951. $10-15.
Crystal with ruby stain #4016-31, 14" 5-part Relish. $75-95.
Crystal with ruby stain #4016-18, 6 3/4" 2-Lite Candleholder. $95-115.
Crystal with ruby stain #4016-1, 9 oz. Goblet. $10-15.
Crystal with ruby stain #4016-7, 4 1/2 oz. Juice Tumbler. $5-10.
Crystal with cranberry stain #4016-20, 5 1/2" Sugar. $20-30.
Crystal with cranberry stain #4016-19, 5" Creamer. $20-30.
Crystal with cranberry stain #4016-4, 2 oz. Wine. $5-10.
Crystal with cranberry stain #4016-9, 8 1/2 oz. Water Tumbler. $10-15.
Crystal with cranberry stain #4016-10, 11 oz. Ice Tea Tumbler. $15-20.
Crystal with cranberry stain #4016-2, 5 1/2 oz. Sundae. $5-10.
#121 Copper decoration, #4016-27, 12 1/2" Flower Floater, c. 1956. $50-70.

King's Crown (Adams). Crystal with ruby stain:
7" h. Tankard Milk Pitcher. $175-225.
11 1/4" h. Tankard Water Pitcher, with Fern and
Berry copper wheel engraving. $275-325.
8 3/8" h. Tankard Milk Pitcher, souvenir piece,
'To My Wife, from Atlantic City 1895.' $200-250.

King's Crown (Adams).
Crystal with ruby stain, 4"
h. Mustard Pot. $475-525.

King's Crown (Adams). Crystal with ruby
stain #9362, 4-Bottle Castor Set.
$650-700 set.

The carrier measures 9" to top of
wire handle, and is 6" wide. The
carrier is only known in Crystal. The
four bottles hold salt, pepper,
mustard and oil/vinegar. Note the
original stopper on the oil/vinegar.
This is the only King's Crown item
that is shown in the 1926 United
States Glass Company catalog. It was
not referred to as King's Crown; it
was given line number #9362.

King's Crown (Adams). Crystal with ruby
stain, 6" Olive Dish. $275-325.

King's Crown (Adams).
Crystal with ruby stain,
10 1/4" Cake Salver.
$775-825.

King's Crown (Adams). Crystal
with ruby stain, Pickle Castor. 8
3/4" h. to top of handle, 4" h.
glass insert. $1100-1300.

King's Crown(Adams). Crystal with ruby stain, Honey Dish. 8" square, 5 1/2" to top of finial. $900-950.

King's Crown (Adams). Crystal with ruby stain:
   8" h. Bulbous Water Pitcher, 2 qt. $350-400.
   6 1/2" Bulbous Milk Pitcher, 1 qt. $300-350.

King's Crown (Adams). Crystal Oil Lamp. 12 3/8" to top of burner. Only known in Crystal. $250-300.

King's Crown. Crystal with ruby stain:
   #4016, 6 3/4" Candleholders. $235-260 pair. This style of candleholder dates from the early 1940s. This shape was adapted from the late 1930s Cascade candleholder mold.
   #4016-38, 12" Straight Edge Bowl. $75-95.

Top: **X.L.C.R. - King's Crown.**
   Crystal with ruby stain, 4 oz. Juice "Souvenir of Tiffin, Ohio." Several of these have been seen, sometimes with the year 1903 added. These would have been produced at Factory A (Adams) in Pittsburgh, and possibly decorated at Tiffin. $35-50.
   Crystal with ruby stain, 4 1/2" h. Spooner, Produced at Factory A. $35-50.
   Milk Glass #4016-30, 6" Candy Box and Cover. Produced at Glassport, c. 1952. $55-75.
   Crystal with sterling mounts #4016 Sugar and Cream. The word Tiffin is imprinted on the outside edge of the silver. Produced at the Glassport factory, c. 1950s. $65-85 pair.

Center: **King's Crown.**
   Crystal #4016-13, 7 3/8" Plate with satin finish on outer band and center. $10-15.
   Crystal #4016-18, 6 3/4" Candleholder with satin finish on candle cups and foot, with painted decoration. $45-65.
   Crystal #4016-13, 7 3/8" Plate with satin finish, gold rim and painted decoration. $15-20.
   There is a 1952 price listing of a King's Crown decoration named Desert Rose. The decoration on these pieces may be that decoration.

King's Crown. Crystal with blue stain
#4016-1, 9 oz. Goblet. $20-25.

Top: Milk Glass #7597 T.V. Snack Set:
   10 1/2" Plate with receptacle;
   #741-14 Old Fashion, 7 oz. decorated #122 (gold). $30-50 set.
Bottom: Crystal #597 T.V. Snack Set:
   10 1/2" Plate with receptacle;
   #4016-10 Ice Tea Tumbler.
   Available in Crystal or Crystal with ruby, blue, cranberry, green, amber and decorated #121, (copper). $45-65 set. These items were introduced in January, 1960, and probably only produced a year or two.

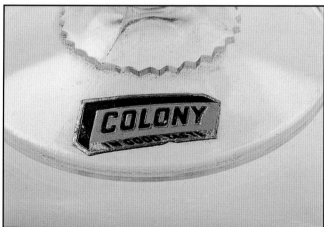

Top: Assortment of Indiana Glass "King's Crown" stems in various colors and decorations, 1959 to present.

Bottom left: Label on Indiana Glass "King's Crown" stem. Indiana Glass is a subsidiary of the Lancaster Colony Corporation. The label reads "Colony, in good taste."

Bottom: **"King's Crown" (Indiana).** Cobalt Blue 3-tier Tidbit Tray. 12 3/4" to top of handle. Indiana Glass produced the cobalt blue color for Tiara Exclusives. Tiara was a division of Indiana Glass. $65-85.

Antique Thumbprint

The Antique Thumbprint line utilized the same molds that were used for King's Crown. Antique Thumbprint was produced in Plum, Golden Banana, Empire Green, and limited production in Cobalt Blue. The only items produced in Cobalt Blue were the stemware and the 7 3/8" plate. Introduced in 1961, Antique Thumbprint was discontinued by the end of 1962.

1961 Antique Thumbprint pamphlet. The colors depicted here are Plum, Golden Banana, and Empire Green.

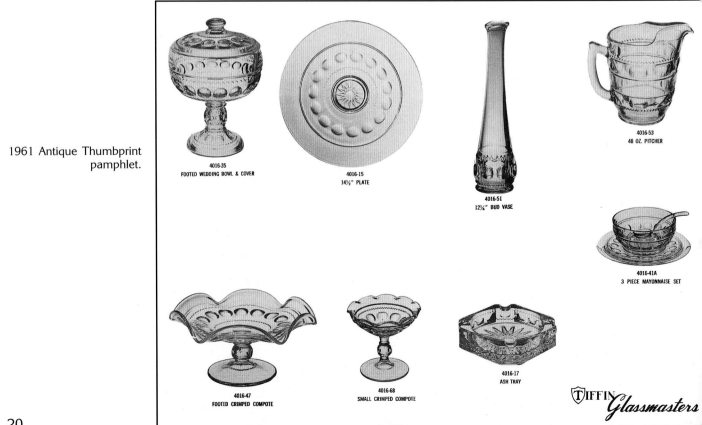

1961 Antique Thumbprint pamphlet.

4016-35
FOOTED WEDDING BOWL & COVER

4016-15
14½" PLATE

4016-51
12¾" BUD VASE

4016-53
48 OZ. PITCHER

4016-41A
3 PIECE MAYONNAISE SET

4016-47
FOOTED CRIMPED COMPOTE

4016-68
SMALL CRIMPED COMPOTE

4016-17
ASH TRAY

TIFFIN Glassmasters

20

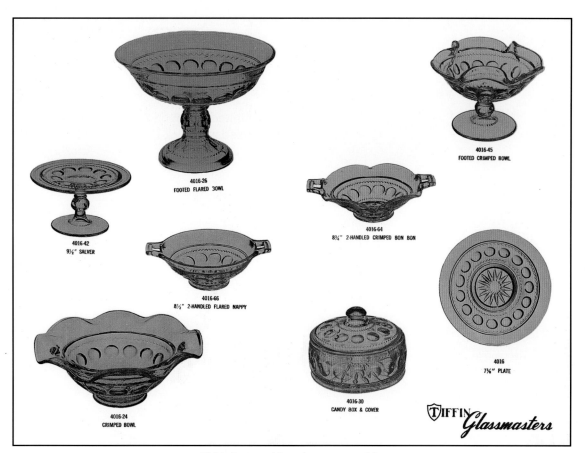

1961 Antique Thumbprint pamphlet.

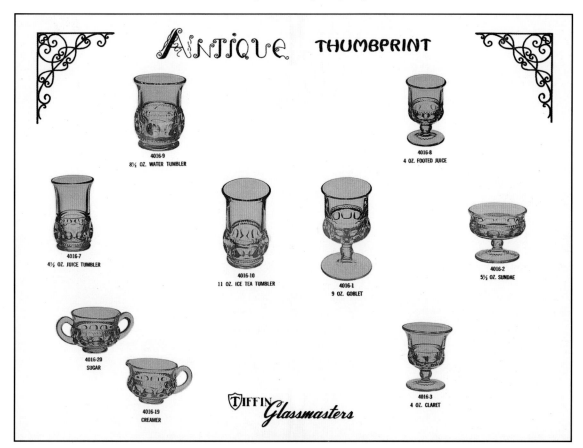

1961 Antique Thumbprint pamphlet.

Antique Thumbprint.
Golden Banana #4016-9, 8 1/2 oz. Water tumbler. $5-10.
Cobalt Blue #4016-13, 3/8" Plate. $10-15.
Cobalt Blue #4016-5, 2 1/4 oz., Cocktail. $10-15.

Antique Thumbprint.
Golden Banana:
#4016-13, 7 3/8" Plate. $5-10.
#4016-15, 14 1/2" Plate. $30-45.
#4016- 41A, 4" Mayonnaise. This is a 3-piece set which should have an underplate, and a Golden Banana color ladle. $15-20.
#4016-19, 5" creamer. $15-20.
#4016-20, 5 1/2" sugar. $15-20.
#4016-68, 4 1/2" h. Small Crimped Compote. $35-45.
#4016-9, 8 1/2" oz. Water Tumbler. $5-10.
#4016-10, 11 oz. Ice Tea Tumbler. $10-15.

Antique Thumbprint. Golden Banana:
 #4016-44, 7 1/2" h. Candy Box and Cover. $55-75.
 #4016-35, 10" h. Footed Wedding Bowl and Cover.
  $75-95.
 #4016-45, 8 1/4" Footed Crimped Bowl. $35-45.
 #4016-30, 6 1/2" Candy Box and Cover. $55-75.
 #4016-66, 8 1/2" 2-Handled Flared Nappy. $35-45.
 #4016-64, 8 3/4" 2-Handled Crimped Bon Bon.
  $35-45

Detail of Antique Thumbprint
pattern.

Antique Thumbprint.
Plum:
#4016-44, 7 1/2" h.
Candy Box and Cover.
$75-95.
#4016-15, 14 1/2"
Plate. $30-45.
#4016-66, 8 1/2" 2-
Handled Flared Nappy.
$35-45.
#4016-53, 7 3/4" h., 48
oz. Jug. $65-85.
#4016-64, 8 3/4" 2-
Handled Crimped Bon
Bon. $35-45.

Antique Thumbprint. Plum:
#4016-7, 4 1/2" oz. Juice Tumbler. $5-10.
#4016-10, 11 oz. Ice Tea Tumbler. $10-15.
#4016-85, 12 3/4" h. Bud Vase. $35-50.
#4016-8, 4 oz. Footed Juice. $5-10.
#4016-26, 12" Footed Flared Bowl. $55-75.
#4016-64, 8 3/4" Crimped Bon Bon. $35-45.
#4016-66, 8 1/2" 2-Handled Flared Nappy. $35-45.
#4016-20, 5 1/2" Sugar. $15-20.
#4016-19, 5" Creamer. $15-20.

Antique Thumbprint.
Plum #4016-42, 9 1/2"
Salver. $50-70.

Antique Thumbprint. Empire Green:
#4016-13, 7 3/8" Plate. $5-10.
#4016-2, 5 1/2 oz. Sundae. $5-10.
#4016-7, 4 1/2 oz. Juice Tumbler. $5-10.
#4016-8, 4 oz. Footed Juice. $5-10.
#4016-20, 5 1/2" Sugar. $15-20.
#4016-19, 5" Creamer. $15-20.

1940 Williamsburg Pamphlet.

308-5
15 in. Plate

THE WILLIAMSBURG
An Open Stock Pattern

HAND-MADE of heavy, crystal clear glass. Both the design and the shapes are adaptations of the 18th century's most popular styles. Designed especially to meet the rapidly growing demand for American historical pieces.

The entire line consists of 100 odd numbers, including baskets, bowls, plates and vases in many sizes, candlesticks in several shapes. Because of the wide variety it is possible to select an entire table service or choose a few matching pieces solely for decorative effect. To select the WILLIAMSBURG pattern is to choose wisely, economically, and in good taste.

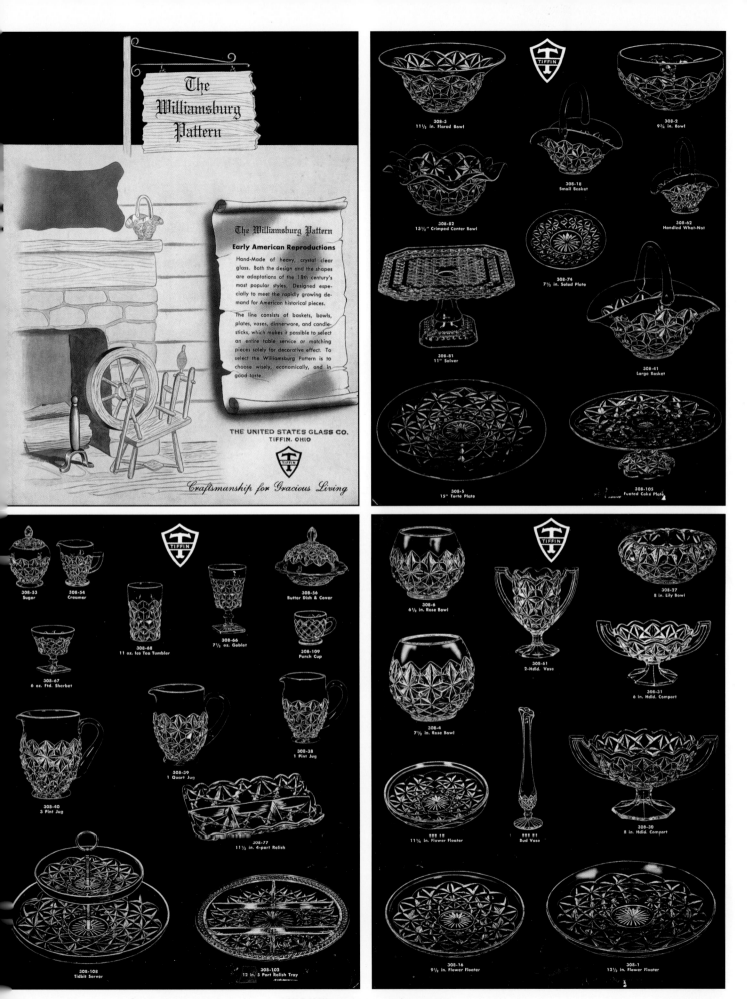

The Williamsburg Pattern

The Williamsburg Pattern

Early American Reproductions

Hand-Made of heavy, crystal clear glass. Both the design and the shapes are adaptations of the 18th century's most popular styles. Designed especially to meet the rapidly growing demand for American historical pieces.

The line consists of baskets, bowls, plates, vases, dinnerware, and candlesticks, which makes it possible to select an entire table service or matching pieces solely for decorative effect. To select the Williamsburg Pattern is to choose wisely, economically, and in good taste.

THE UNITED STATES GLASS CO.
TIFFIN, OHIO

Craftsmanship for Gracious Living

308-3
11½ in. Flared Bowl

308-2
9¾ in. Bowl

308-18
Small Basket

308-82
13½" Crimped Center Bowl

308-62
Handled What-Not

308-74
7½ in. Salad Plate

308-81
11" Salver

308-41
Large Basket

308-5
15" Torte Plate

308-105
Footed Cake Plate

308-53
Sugar

308-54
Creamer

308-56
Butter Dish & Cover

308-68
11 oz. Ice Tea Tumbler

308-66
7½ oz. Goblet

308-109
Punch Cup

308-67
6 oz. Ftd. Sherbet

308-38
1 Pint Jug

308-39
1 Quart Jug

308-40
3 Pint Jug

308-77
11½ in. 4-part Relish

308-108
Tidbit Server

308-102
12 in. 5 Part Relish Tray

308-6
6½ in. Rose Bowl

308-27
8 in. Lily Bowl

308-61
2-Hdld. Vase

308-31
6 in. Hdld. Compart

308-4
7½ in. Rose Bowl

308-30
8 in. Hdld. Compart

308-... in. Flower Floater

Bud Vase

308-16
9½ in. Flower Floater

308-1
13½ in. Flower Floater

1956 Williamsburg catalog pages.

Williamsburg. Crystal with ruby stain #308-109 Tidbit Server. $75-95.

Williamsburg. Crystal:
  #308-105, 13 1/2" Footed Cake Plate. $45-65.
  #308-41, 11 3/4" Large Basket. $45-65.
  #308-66, 7 1/2 oz. Goblet. $5-10.
  The May, 1994 issue of "The Daze" shows a photograph of
  new offerings from the L.E. Smith Glass Company of
  Mount Pleasant, PA. The photo shows three items that
  they have reproduced from United States Glass Company
  Williamsburg pattern molds; the #308-82 Crimped
  Center B owl, the #308-20 Scalloped Edge Bowl and the
  #308-5, 15" Plate. L.E. Smith marketed these three items
  as part of their Solitaire Collection.

Williamsburg. Crystal with ruby stain:
  #308-63, 8" Small Oval Fruit. $30-40.
  #308-65, 12" Large Oval Fruit. $35-45.
  #308-4, 7 1/2" h. Rose Bowl. $40-60.
  The oval fruits are the baskets without handles.

Williamsburg

The #308 pattern was introduced by United States Glass Company c. 1926, without much success. It was reintroduced in 1940 as Williamsburg. The name was apparently chosen to capitalize on the Colonial Revival style, which was popular at that time. Charleston and Virginian are two other lines from the same time frame with a colonial-themed name. The Williamsburg line consisted of over a hundred items, with a limited number of items in ruby or cranberry stain. Thirteen items were offered in Milk Glass in a 1952 price listing. In 1961, a very limited number of items were offered in Plum, Golden Banana, Empire Green, and Cobalt Blue. The handled whatnot

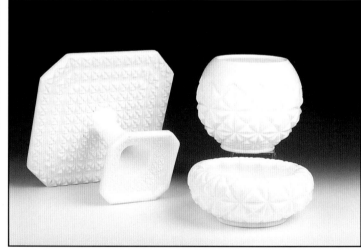

Williamsburg. Milk Glass:
  #708-80, 11" Square Salver. $40-60.
  #708-4, 7 1/2" h. Rose bowl. $35-55.
  #708-27, 8" Lily Bowl. $30-50.

and small basket were produced in the Tiffin Rose color in 1962.

The Indiana Glass Company has reproduced the Williamsburg pattern as Monticello. Many of the shapes are the same as Tiffin's, while a few new pieces were also made, such as the square basket. Known Indiana Glass colors are orange, blue, green, amberina, teal, and milk glass. Some of these colors can be found with a satin finish.

Williamsburg. Milk Glass:
   #708-58, 6" h., Celery Vase. $25-45.
   #708-57, 4 1/4", 2-Handled Footed Salt Dips.
   $15-25 each.

Williamsburg.
   Milk Glass #708-4, 7 1/2" h. Rose Bowl. $35-55.
   Crystal with allover gold decoration #308-62, 5
   3/4" Handled What Not. $45-65.

Williamsburg.
   Milk Glass #708-39, 6 1/4" h. One Quart Jug.
   $30-50.
   Milk Glass #708-61, 7" h. Handled Urn Vase.
   $20-30.
   Crystal with allover gold decoration #308-31,
   6" Handled Compote. $45-65.

Williamsburg.
Crystal with ruby stain #308-77, 11 1/4" 4-part Relish. $30-45. Crystal with ruby stain #308-5, 15" Torte Plate. $30-45.

Williamsburg. Empire Green #308-30, 8" Handled Compote. The Williamsburg pattern is very hard to find in the Empire Green color. $65-85.

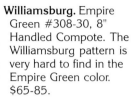

Williamsburg.
Upper Two Rows: #308-18, 9" Small Baskets.
   Plum. $65-85.
   Golden Banana. $65-85.
   Tiffin Rose. $90-110.
Bottom Row: #308-62, 5 3/4" Handled What Nots.
   Plum. $55-75.
   Cobalt Blue with Crystal trim. $100-120.
   Golden Banana. $55-75.
   Tiffin Rose. $80-100.

Williamsburg.
    Golden Banana #308-30, 8" Handled Compote. $50-70.
    Golden Banana #308-31, 6" Handled Compote. $45-65.
    Plum #308-30, 8" Handled Compote. $50-70.
    Golden Banana #308-39, 6 1/4" h. One-Quart Jug. $45-65.
    Plum #308-94, 9" h. Bud Vase. $25-45.
    Golden Banana #308-94, 9" h. Bud Vase. $25-45.

Detail of Williamsburg basket handle prunt. The prunt has a "pinwheel" design. The crystal Williamsburg baskets have no prunts.

Detail of Indiana Glass "Monticello" basket handle prunt. The square style baskets, and the large flared baskets all have this style of "5-dot" prunt. This style of prunt is also used on baskets in other Indiana Glass lines.

Indiana Glass. Colors used by Indiana Glass on the two-handled urn vase. Indiana Glass called their reproduction of the Williamsburg line, Monticello. The Indiana Glass colors all differ from Tiffin's; however, both companies produced items in milk glass.

Indiana Glass. Assortment of colors shown on the Monticello pattern, Indiana Glass baskets.

Opposite page, top left, top right & bottom left: 1942 Charleston Catalog page.
Bottom right: August 1946 China and Glass advertisement for the Charleston pattern. Note the different style of cream and sugar than those shown in the catalog pages.

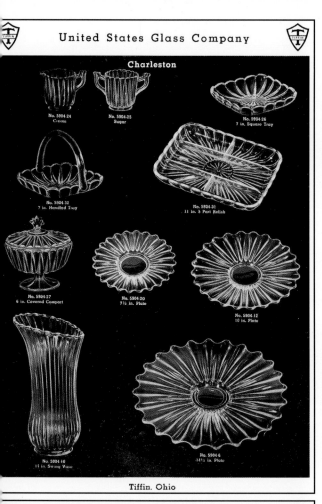

Charleston

No. 5904-24
Cream

No. 5904-25
Sugar

No. 5904-26
7 in. Square Tray

No. 5904-32
7 in. Handled Tray

No. 5904-31
11 in. 5 Part Relish

No. 5904-27
6 in. Covered Comport

No. 5904-20
7½ in. Plate

No. 5904-12
10 in. Plate

No. 5904-10
11 in. Swing Vase

No. 5904-6
14½ in. Plate

Tiffin, Ohio

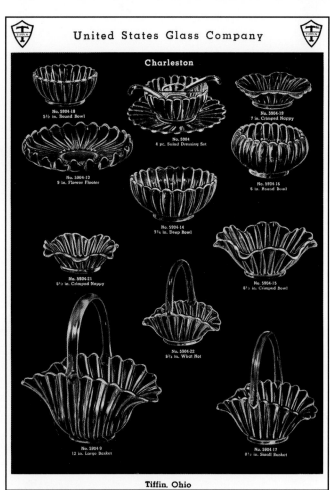

Charleston

No. 5904-18
5½ in. Round Bowl

No. 5904
4 pc. Salad Dressing Set

No. 5904-19
7 in. Crimped Nappy

No. 5904-13
9 in. Flower Floater

No. 5904-16
6 in. Round Bowl

No. 5904-14
7¾ in. Deep Bowl

No. 5904-21
5½ in. Crimped Nappy

No. 5904-15
8½ in. Crimped Bowl

No. 5904-22
8¾ in. What Not

No. 5904-9
12 in. Large Basket

No. 5904-17
8½ in. Small Basket

Tiffin, Ohio

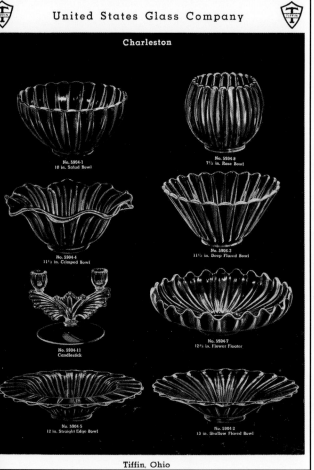

Charleston

No. 5904-1
10 in. Salad Bowl

No. 5904-8
7½ in. Rose Bowl

No. 5904-4
11½ in. Crimped Bowl

No. 5904-3
11½ in. Deep Flared Bowl

No. 5904-11
Candlestick

No. 5904-7
12½ in. Flower Floater

No. 5904-5
12 in. Straight Edge Bowl

No. 5904-2
13 in. Shallow Flared Bowl

Tiffin, Ohio

CHARLESTON...

An elegant simplicity distinguishes this charming petal-pattern — *Charleston*. Like the lovely flower which inspired its design, *Charleston* is graciously at home in every setting — traditional or modern. Hand-crafted...Hand-finished...in gem-bright glass of rich weight...*Charleston* possesses in generous measure both functional and decorative value. It has a precious look of costliness, yet it is priced for the budget-minded. *Charleston* is destined for wide demand.

UNITED STATES GLASS CO. • • • TIFFIN, OHIO

1942 Charleston catalog pages.

Charleston

The Charleston #5904 line was introduced c. 1942, and was produced in Crystal at the Glassport factory. A 1942 advertisement described it as a deeply fluted colonial design. There are about fifty items in the Charleston line, and the design somewhat resembles Heisey's Crystolite pattern. Charleston was also featured in a 1947 advertisement, so the line must have been fairly successful, with about a five-year production run.

Charleston. Crystal with satin finish, and painted decoration:
    #5904-20, 7 1/2" Plate. $10-20.
    #5904-6, 14 1/2" Plate. $20-30.
    #5904-12, 10" Plate. $15-25.
    Crystal #5904-7, 12 1/2" Flower Floater. $20-30.

The United States Glass Co.'s new "Virginian" design in pressed crystal is represented at the right by two of a wide range of pieces. The rayed design lends itself well either to flared or cupped modelings.

February 1942 China and Glass advertisement for the Virginian pattern.

Virginian

The #5903 Virginian pattern was introduced c. 1942 in Crystal, and was produced at the Glassport factory. Virginian utilizes the same basic shapes as the Charleston line, with the addition of a series of embossed circles on the rays of the glassware. Produced in about fifty items, Virginian is a look-alike to the pattern Columbia, manufactured by the Federal Glass Company from 1938 to 1942.

Baronial

The Baronial #6859 line, is a United States Glass Company pressed tableware pattern introduced as early as 1924 with production through about 1930. This line was produced at the Glassport factory in Rose Pink and Reflex Green. Early production also consisted of Crystal, and Crystal with ruby stain. Baronial was reissued in 1941, this time to lukewarm response. A large Crystal basket was offered in 1941.

Baronial. Crystal with ruby stain #6859, 8 1/4" h. Candlesticks. $100-125 pair.

Top left: April 1941 issue of China, Glass and Lamps promoting the new Baronial basket.

Bottom left: 1926 United States Glass Company catalog page featuring the Baronial pattern. Produced at Factory G, Glassport.

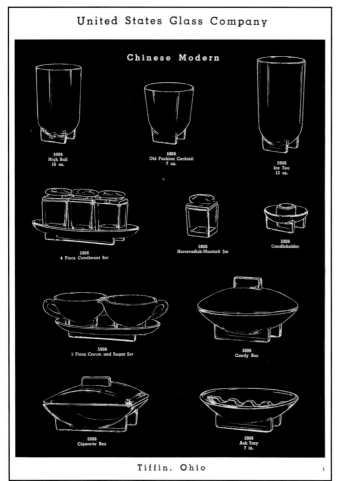

United States Glass Company

Chinese Modern

5906
High Ball
10 oz.

5906
Old Fashion Cocktail
7 oz.

5906
Ice Tea
12 oz.

5906
4 Piece Condiment Set

5906
Horseradish-Mustard Jar

5906
Candleholder

5906
3 Piece Cream and Sugar Set

5906
Candy Box

5906
Cigarette Box

5906
Ash Tray
7 in.

Tiffin, Ohio

1

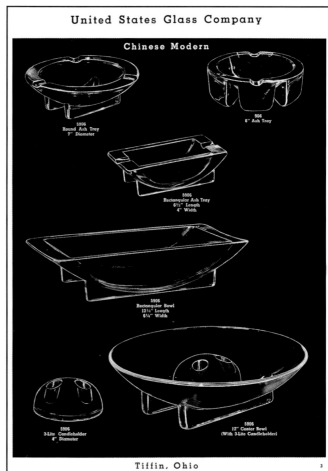

United States Glass Company

Chinese Modern

5906
Round Ash Tray
7" Diameter

906
6" Ash Tray

5906
Rectangular Ash Tray
6½" Length
4" Width

5906
Rectangular Bowl
12¼" Length
6¼" Width

5906
3-Lite Candleholder
4" Diameter

5906
12" Center Bowl
(With 3-Lite Candleholder)

Tiffin, Ohio

3

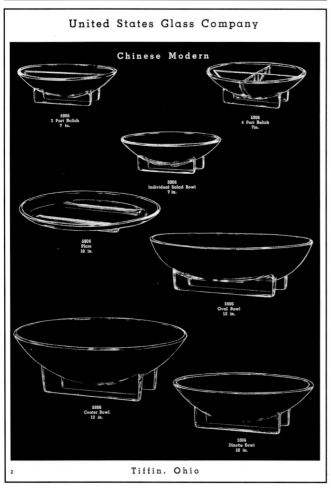

United States Glass Company

Chinese Modern

5906
2 Part Relish
7 in.

5906
4 Part Relish
7in.

5906
Individual Salad Bowl
7 in.

5906
Plate
10 in.

5906
Oval Bowl
12 in.

5906
Center Bowl
12 in.

5906
Dinette Bowl
10 in.

Tiffin, Ohio

2

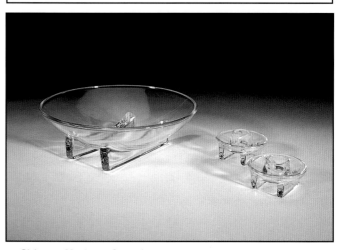

Chinese Modern. Crystal:
#5906, 10" Dinette Bowl. $35-55.
#5906, 3" Candleholders. $35-55 pair.

Top left, bottom left & top right: 1956 Chinese Modern catalog page.

Chinese Modern

Introduced in the late 1940s, Chinese Modern was a pressed tableware line, #5906, produced at the Glassport factory. This line was available through about 1962. Most production was in Crystal, and Crystal with platinum trim. The rectangular ash tray, and the cigarette box were available in 1960 in an allover gold decoration.

Pearl Edge

The Pearl Edge #5909 line was introduced in May, 1949, in Crystal, with the color Killarney added in November of that year. Pearl Edge is a tableware line of about 30 items including several different center bowls, two styles of creams and sugars, finger bowl, nappy, salad plate, berry set, bread tray, mayonnaise bowl, and center handled cake plate. Killarney is the more collectible of the two colors. Crystal is seldom collected, unless it has an etching. The June Night, Cherokee Rose, Fuchsia, Tiffin or Rambling Rose, Springtime and Cerise etchings can be found on Crystal blanks. Collectors of these etchings will often pay a premium price for these items, because they are quite hard to find.

March 1949 Crockery and Glass Journal advertisement for the Pearl Edge line.

May 1949 Crockery and Glass Journal advertisement for the Pearl Edge line.

Pearl Edge. Killarney:
#5909-10, 8 1/4" Oblong Bread Tray. $30-40
#5909-18, 12" Center Handled Cake Plate. $65-85
#5909-17, 4" Creamer, 4 1/2" Sugar. $40-60 set.
#5909-20, 10 1/2", 2-Handled Berry Bowl. $40-60.

#5909-14, Mayonnaise Set, 5 1/4" Bowl, 6 1/2" plate. $40-60 set.
#5909-7, 12 1/2" Oval Relish. $50-70.
#5909-28, 4 1/2" Sugar, 4" Creamer. $50-70 set.

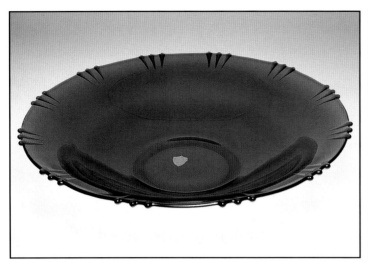

Pearl Edge. Killarney #5909-2, 13" Center Bowl. $50-70.

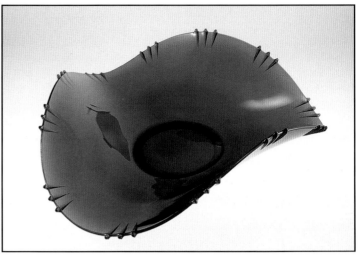

Pearl Edge. Killarney #5909-5, 13" Fruit Bowl. $55-75.

Pearl Edge. Crystal:
   #5909-28, 4 1/2" Sugar, 4" Creamer. $75-95 set .
   #5909-8, 12" Center Handled Cake Plate. $300-325.
   #5909-14, 5 1/4" Mayonnaise Bowl. $50-70.
   #5909-25, 10" 2-Lite Candlestick. $200-225.
   #5909-7, 12 1/2" Oval Relish. $125-150.
   #5909-10, 8 1/2" Oblong Bread Tray. $90-110.
   All items have the Fuchsia etching, except for the center handled
   cake plate, which has the June Night etching.

Lancelot. Crystal:
#5911, 9 7/8" 2-Lite Candleholders. $100-125 set.
#5911, 11 3/4" Center Bowl. $45-65.

January 1949 Crockery and Glass Journal advertisement for the Lancelot pattern.

September 1948 Crockery and Glass Journal advertisement for the Lancelot pattern.

Lancelot

Lancelot, #5911, is a seldom seen pattern that was introduced in 1948 in a limited number of items. Four sizes of stems, a compote, cream and sugar, 5-part relish, 2-lite candleholders, dessert plate, and a mayonnaise bowl were offered. Only items in Crystal have been seen, but other colors or decorations are possible.

Betsy Ross

The tableware line known today as Betsy Ross, was called Queen Anne when it was introduced c. 1922 by the United States Glass Company. Queen Anne was reissued as Betsy Ross, #15309, in 1934. In the early 1940s, a number of the molds were reworked, and the line underwent yet another name change. The line was renamed Pinafore, with production only in Crystal. The line number for Pinafore was changed from #15309 to #15367. In 1957, a number of items were produced in Milk Glass, and were advertised as Betsy Ross once again. The line number for the Milk Glass items is #709. Four items were offered in Empire Green, Plum and Golden Banana in 1961; a compote, two-handled vase, footed candy box with cover and a three-toed handled nappy. The line number was changed yet again for these four items, to #509.

Top right: 1926 United States Glass Company catalog page showing the Queen Anne pattern, renamed Betsy Ross in 1934. Produced at Factory G, Glassport.

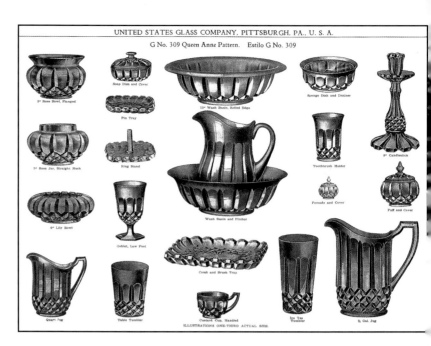

1926 United States Glass Company catalog page.

1926 United States Glass Company catalog page.

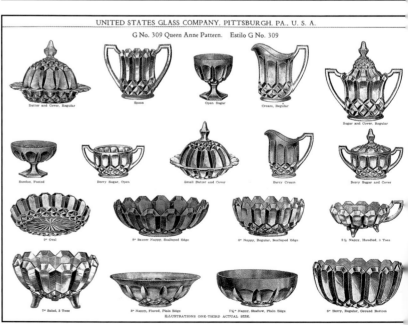

Pinafore. Crystal:
    #15367, 7" h. Candlesticks. $65-85
    pair.
    #15367, 12" Centerpiece Bowl. $30-50.

Betsy Ross. Milk Glass:
    #709-17, 6" Compote. $25-40.
    #709-5, 7 1/2" 3-toed Bowl. $25-40.

Early 1940s pamphlet showing the
pieces available in the Pinafore pattern.

Pinafore.

41

Top left: **Betsy Ross**. Milk Glass:
  #709-16, 10" Vase. $30-50.
  #709-17, 6" Compote. $25-40.

Top right: **Betsy Ross**.
  Plum #509-4, 7 1/2" Urn Vase. $45-65.
  Plum #509-12, 9 1/2" Footed Candy Box and Cover. $100-125.
  Golden Banana #509-12, 9 1/2" Footed Candy Box and Cover.
   $100-125.

Front Cover of the March 15, 1957 issue of the Crockery and Glass Journal promoting the Betsy Ross line. Note that Betsy Ross is being marketed within the Duncan and Miller Division of the United States Glass Company. Betsy Ross was an original United States Glass Company line from the 1920s.

Grape

The Grape, #519 pattern was a re-issue of the Palm Beach pattern. The Palm Beach design was originally a United States Glass Company line dating from about 1909. Palm Beach was produced in Crystal, Crystal with decoration, Blue Opalescent, Canary Opalescent and Carnival colors. The Grape pattern in Milk Glass was produced in 1957 at the Glassport factory; the Palm Beach design had also been manufactured at Glassport.

In 1961 four items were offered in Plum or Golden Banana; a vase, nappy, crimped bowl, and tumbler. These items were produced at the Tiffin factory.

Top right: **Grape.** Milk Glass:
    #719-7, 8 oz. Tumbler. $10-15.
    #719-6, 52 oz. Jug. $45-65.
    #719-8, 7 oz. Cream. $25-35.
    #719-9, 7 oz. Sugar and Cover. $25-35.
    #719-12, 8", 1/2 lb. Butter and Cover. $65-85.

Grape. Milk Glass:
    #719-1, 7 1/2" Nappy. $20-30.
    #719-4, 4 1/2" Nappy. $15-25.
    #719-13, 7 1/2" Pickle. $15-25.

Detail of Grape pattern.

Grape. Milk Glass #719-11, 6" h.
Vase. $25-40.

Top right: Bullseye.
   Golden Banana #15078, 10 1/4" Cake Salver.
   $100-125.
   Crystal with ruby stain, #15078, 9 1/4" Cake
   Salver. $100-125.
   The Bullseye cake salver was available in three
   sizes in Crystal: 10 1/4", 9 1/4" and 8". These
   were offered in all Crystal, or Crystal with ruby,
   cranberry, or blue stain.

Top left: Grape.
   Golden Banana #519-14, 7" Crimped Bowl.
   $35-55.
   Golden Banana #519-11, 6" h. Vase. $35-55.
   Golden Banana #519-7, 8 oz. Tumbler. $10-15.
   Plum #519-11, 6" h. Vase. $35-55.
   Plum #519-14, 7" Crimped Bowl. $35-55.
   Plum #519-1, 7 1/2" Nappy. $35-55.

Center: Bullseye.
   Golden Banana #15078, 10 1/4" Cake Salver.
   $100-125.
   Plum #15078, 10 1/4" Cake Salver. $100-125.

Bullseye

The Bullseye, #15078 line, is an early
United States Glass Company pattern. It was
produced at the Glassport factory c. 1902
and was called Manhattan, the name known
by most collectors today. A punch set, nappy,
straw jar, and cracker jar were offered in the
early 1940s, and this is possibly when the
design was renamed Bullseye. The punch
set was available in Crystal and Crystal with
ruby stain. In the early 1950s, a cake salver
was available in Crystal with ruby stain. Three
sizes of cake salvers were offered in the late
1950s: 8", 9 1/4" and 10 1/4". These were
available in Crystal or Crystal with ruby, cranberry or blue stain. In 1961, the 10 1/4" cake
salver was available in the Plum and Golden
Banana colors. These were produced at the
Tiffin factory.

Detail of Bullseye pattern.

Loop and Punty.
Golden Banana #1961-35, 5 1/4" Footed
  Sugar. $20-30.
Golden Banana #1961-36, 4 3/4" Footed
  Cream. $20-30.
Golden Banana #1961-39, 6" Nappy. $20-30.
Golden Banana #1961-41, 6" 2-compartment
  Mayonnaise Bowl. $20-30.
Plum #1961-38, 4 3/4" Nappy. $15-25.
Cobalt Blue #1961-11, Water Tumbler. $15-25.

.oop and Punty.
Golden Banana #1961-35, 5 1/4" Footed Sugar.
  $20-30.
Cobalt Blue #1961-11, Water Tumbler. $15-25.
Plum #1961-38, 4 3/4" Nappy. $15-25.
Crystal #1961-28, 14" Plate. $15-25.
Crystal #1961-31, 12" Flower Floater. $15-25.
Crystal #1961-10, Ice Tea Tumbler. $10-15.

Loop and Punty

The Loop and Punty, #1961 line, was
introduced in nineteen items in August,
1961, in Golden Banana, Plum, and Cobalt Blue. Items can also occasionally be
found in Crystal. By January, 1962, selec-
tion was limited to six items in the afore-
mentioned colors. One intriguing item
listed was a footed fruit and flower epergne.

Antique

The #15150 line was a complete tableware line which was produced at Factory U, located at Gas City, Indiana, as early as 1915. A punch set was shown in a 1940 United States Glass Company catalog listed as Antique. In 1962, an 8" footed bowl was offered in Plum and Golden Banana and the line was renumbered #565-1.

Detail of Antique pattern.

Antique. Golden Banana #565-1, 8" Footed Bowl. $65-85.

Top right: United States Glass Company, Factory U, 1915 catalog page featuring the #15150 line. Factory U was located at Gas City, Indiana. The punch set was produced in 1940 as the Antique pattern at Factory G. In 1962, the 8" footed compote was produced in the Plum and Golden Banana colors at Factory R.

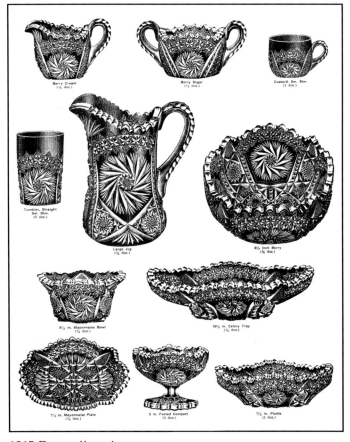

1915 Factory U catalog page.

1915 Factory U catalog page.

Chapter 2
Duncan and Miller Division Pressed Patterns

After the closing of the Duncan and Miller Glass Company, located in Washington, Pennsylvania, many of their molds and equipment were purchased by the United States Glass Company in 1955. A Duncan and Miller division of the United States Glass Company was established in 1956 and was headed by James Duncan. Products included several old United States Glass Company patterns and reproductions from a number of the Duncan and Miller molds. Production took place at the Tiffin and Glassport factories. The Duncan and Miller Division ceased to be used as a marketing tool, after the United States Glass Company went bankrupt in 1963. A number of the Duncan and Miller patterns continued to be produced by Tiffin Glass until the factory closed in 1980. The Homestead, Swirl, and Georgian pattern names were not used by Tiffin Glass. We are including them here under the original Duncan and Miller names as a means of identification.

THE CANTERBURY LINE

Tiffin Canterbury . . . its clean lines and classic proportions make it suitable for traditional or modern decor.

1968 Canterbury catalog page.

Canterbury

Tiffin reproduced glassware using many of the Canterbury molds acquired from the Duncan and Miller Glass Company. The main color production was in Crystal, but several other colors can be found as well: Copen Blue, Smoke, Persimmon, Citron Green, Wild Rose, Greenbriar, Desert Red, Flame, Black, and Dawn (Twilight). The color name Dawn was substituted for Twilight when a Duncan and Miller mold was used, and the number nine was added as a prefix to the line number. At the same time, the color Twilight was being used for items produced from Tiffin molds. An easy way to identify the correct color names and molds is: Dawn = Duncan, and Twilight = Tiffin. The first letters of the color and company names are the same. Tiffin used the term Dawn from about 1957-1963. Items produced after 1963 from Duncan and Miller molds in the Twilight color, were referred to as Twilight; the color name Dawn was no longer used. A 1963 price listing shows three items available in the Flame color: the #115-52 6" relish, the #115-79 32 oz. martini mixer, and the #115-113 flower arranger. These items are extremely scarce.

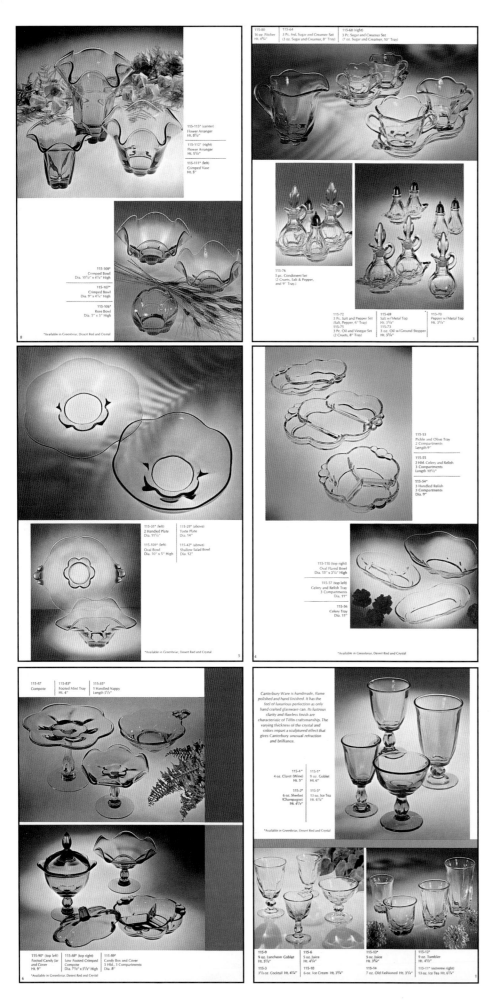

115-113* (center)
Flower Arranger
Ht. 8¾"

115-112* (right)
Flower Arranger
Ht. 5½"

115-111* (left)
Crimped Vase
Ht. 5"

115-108*
Crimped Bowl
Dia. 10½" x 4¼" High

115-107*
Crimped Bowl
Dia. 9" x 4¼" High

115-106*
Rose Bowl
Dia. 5" x 3" High

8   *Available in Greenbriar, Desert Red and Crystal

115-80
16 oz. Pitcher
Ht. 4¾"

115-64
3 Pc. Ind. Sugar and Creamer Set
(3 oz. Sugar and Creamer, 8" Tray)

115-68 (right)
3 Pc. Sugar and Creamer Set
(7 oz. Sugar and Creamer, 10" Tray)

115-76
5 pc. Condiment Set
(2 Cruets, Salt & Pepper,
and 9" Tray.)

115-72
3 Pc. Salt and Pepper Set
(Salt, Pepper, 6" Tray)

115-75
3 Pc. Oil and Vinegar Set
(2 Cruets, 8" Tray)

115-69
Salt w/Metal Top
Ht. 3¼"

115-73
3 oz. Oil w/Ground Stopper
Ht. 5⅝"

115-70
Pepper w/Metal Top
Ht. 3¼"

3

115-53
Pickle and Olive Tray
2 Compartments
Length 9"

115-55
2 Hbl. Celery and Relish
3 Compartments
Length 10½"

115-54*
3 Handled Relish
3 Compartments
Dia. 9"

1968 Canterbury catalog pages.

115-31* (left)
2 Handled Plate
Dia. 11½"

115-29* (above)
Torte Plate
Dia. 14"

115-103* (left)
Oval Bowl
Dia. 10" x 5" High

115-42* (above)
Shallow Salad Bowl
Dia. 12"

115-110 (top right)
Oval Flared Bowl
Dia. 13" x 3¾" High

115-57 (top left)
Celery and Relish Tray
3 Compartments
Dia. 11"

115-56
Celery Tray
Dia. 11"

*Available in Greenbriar, Desert Red and Crystal

5   4

115-87
Compote

115-83*
Footed Mint Tray
Ht. 4"

115-85*
1 Handled Nappy
Length 5½"

Canterbury Ware is handmade, flame
polished and hand finished. It has the
feel of luxurious perfection as only
hand crafted glassware can. Its lustrous
clarity and flawless finish are
characteristic of Tiffin craftsmanship. The
varying thickness of the crystal and
colors impart a sculptured effect that
gives Canterbury unusual refraction
and brilliance.

115-4*
4 oz. Claret (Wine)
Ht. 5"

115-1*
9 oz. Goblet
Ht. 6"

115-2*
6 oz. Sherbet
(Champagne)
Ht. 4½"

115-5*
13 oz. Ice Tea
Ht. 6¼"

*Available in Greenbriar, Desert Red and Crystal

115-90* (top left)
Footed Candy Jar
and Cover
Ht. 9"

115-88* (top right)
Low Footed Crimped
Compote
Dia. 7½" x 5½" High

115-89*
Candy Box and Cover
3 Hbd., 3 Compartments
Dia. 8"

*Available in Greenbriar, Desert Red and Crystal

6

115-9
9 oz. Luncheon Goblet
Ht. 5½"

115-3
3½ oz. Cocktail Ht. 4¼"

115-6
5 oz. Juice
Ht. 4½"

115-10
6 oz. Ice Cream Ht. 3½"

115-13*
9 oz. Tumbler
Ht. 3¾"

115-14
7 oz. Old Fashioned Ht. 3¾"

115-12*
13 oz. Tumbler
Ht. 4½"

115-11* (extreme right)
13 oz. Ice Tea Ht. 6¼"

1

48

1968 Canterbury catalog page.

| 115-28 Dinner Plate Dia. 11" | 115-26" Plate Dia. 7½" |
| 115-32 6 oz. Cup and Saucer Dia. Saucer 6" | 115-16 Dessert Dish (Fingerbowl) Ht. 2", Dia. 4¼" |

| 115-51 4 Pc. Salad Dressing Set (2 Ladles, 5" Bowl, 7½" Plate) | 115-49 3 Pc. Ftd. Mayo Set Bowl: 5" Diameter Plate: 7½" Diameter | 115-84* Fruit Nappy Dia. 5" |

*Available in Greenbriar, Desert Red and Crystal

Canterbury.
Cobalt Blue #115-94, 4 1/2" Club Ash Tray. $45-65.
Copen Blue #115-93, 3" Club Ash Tray. $15-20.

Detail of base of the Canterbury design.

Canterbury. Copen Blue:
#115-106, 5" Rose Bowl. $45-65.
#115-90, 9" h. Footed Candy Jar and Cover. $75-95.
#115-122, 7" 2-Lite Candlestick. $45-65.
#115-84, 5" Fruit Nappy. $15-20.
#115-113, 8 1/2" Flower Arranger. $65-85.
#115-111, 5" h. Crimped Vase. $25-35.
#115-109, 10" Oval Bowl, satin finish. $35-50.
#115-1, 9 oz. Goblet. $15-20.

Canterbury. Dawn:
  #9115-106, 5" Rose Bowl. $65-85.
  #9115-88, 7 1/2" Low Footed Compote. $65-85.
  #9115-108, 10 1/2" Crimped Bowl. $65-85.
  #9115-90, 9" h. Footed Candy Jar and Cover.
   $100-125.
  #9115-122, 7" 2-Lite Candlestick. $100-125.
  #9115-65, 7 oz. Sugar. $45-65.
  #9115-66, 7 oz. Cream. $45-65.

Canterbury. Wild Rose:
  #115-94, 4 1/2" Club Ash Tray. $35-50.
  #115-54, 9" 3-Handled Relish. $35-50.
  #115-97, 4 1/2" Rectangular Ash Tray. $15-20.
  Canterbury production in the Wild Rose color is
   very limited.

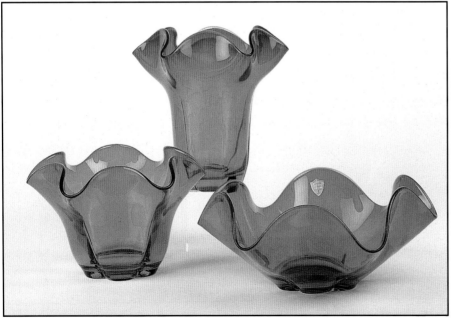

Canterbury. Persimmon:
  #115-112, 5 1/2" h. Flower Arranger. $25-45.
  #115-113, 8 1/2" h. Flower Arranger. $30-50.
  #115-108, 10 1/2" Crimped Bowl. $25-45.
  Canterbury production in Persimmon was
   limited.

nterbury.
Smoke #115-4, 4 oz. Claret or Wine. $5-10.
Greenbrier #115-1, 9 oz. Goblet. $5-10.
Citron Green #115-89, 8" Candy Box and Cover.
  $25-45.
Desert Red #115-1, 9 oz. Goblet. $5-10.
Citron Green #115-121, 3" h. Low Candlesticks.
  $25-45 pair.
Citron Green #155-1, 9 oz. Goblet. $5-10.

Canterbury.
  Greenbriar with satin finish #115-106, 5" Rose
    Bowl. $10-20.
  Smoke #115-106, 5" Rose Bowl. $15-25.
  Citron Green #115-106, 5" Rose Bowl. $25-45.

nterbury. Clockwise from lower left:
Greenbriar #115-106, 5" Rose Bowl. $10-20.
Copen Blue #115-109, 10" Oval Bowl. $35-50.
Desert Red #115-42, 12" Shallow Salad Bowl.
  $20-30.
Greenbriar #115-107, 9" Crimped Bowl. $15-25.
Desert Red #115-54, 9" 3-Handled Relish. $15-25.
  All items with satin finish.

Canterbury. Crystal:
  #115-29, 14" Torte
  Plate. $90-110.
  #115-107, 9" Crimped
  Bowl. $100-125.
  #115-58, 12" Celery
  and Relish. $100-125.
  All items with Fuchsia
  etching.

Canterbury. Black #115-54, 8" 3-Handled Relish. $25-45. Very
limited production of Canterbury in Black.

C. 1970 interior shot of the Tiffin Glass Outlet Store. In the foreground are
items in Canterbury in Crystal, Smoke, Greenbriar, and Copen Blue.

C. 1970 interior shot of the Tiffin Glass Outlet Store, showing many pieces of
Canterbury in Smoke and Crystal. Notice the non-Tiffin items including the tall
green vases, and the shorter orange vase.

C. 1970 interior shot of the Tiffin Glass Outlet Store. Note the Greenbriar and Desert Red ash trays and the non-Tiffin items on the right hand side of the table.

C. 1970 interior shot of the Tiffin Glass Outlet Store. Note the non-Tiffin items in the foreground, which disproves the common conception that everything purchased at the Outlet Store was a Tiffin Glass product.

C. 1970 photograph of the Big Top Glass Sale held in front of the Tiffin Glass factory on Vine Street, to help reduce inventory.

C. 1970 photograph of the interior of the Big Top Glass Sale. Note the Tiffin Glass Smoke and Crystal stemware. The tall orange and blue and crystal vases are not Tiffin Glass items.

Sandwich

The #41 Sandwich tableware line proved to be very successful for Tiffin Glass. The actual name of the line is Early American Sandwich Glass; later U.S. Glass price lists simply called it Sandwich, and that is the name used by collectors. Reproduced in about 100 items, in Crystal, from the original Duncan and Miller molds, Sandwich was made from 1957 to 1963. The only color production of Sandwich took place in 1961. The #41-102 candy jar, and the #41-103 bon bon were made in Plum, Golden Banana and Empire Green. All of the Crystal ware was made at Glassport, and the colored ware at Tiffin.

Sandwich. Crystal #14-107, 14" h. Footed Fruit and Flower Epergne. $175-200.

Sandwich. Crystal #41-81 Cheese and Cracker 2-piece set: Plate 13", Cheese Stand 5 1/2". $45-65 set.

Sandwich. Crystal #41-74, 5-Piece Condiment Set: Vinegar and Oil 5 3/4" h., Small Salt and Pepper 2 1/2" h., Tray 8". $85-115 set.

White Lace. Milk Glass #741-121, 4" h. 1-Lite candlestick. $15-25.
Sandwich. Crystal:
#41-124, 10" h. 1-Lite Candelabra. $90-110.
#41-122, 7 3/4" 2-Lite Candlestick. $45-65.

Sandwich.
Golden Banana #41-102, 8 1/2" h. Candy Jar and Cover. $55-75.
Plum #41-103, 7 1/4" h. Footed Bon Bon and Cover. $50-70.

Indiana Glass. Sandwich pieces reproduced by Indiana Glass. The Indiana Glass colors for this line differ from the Tiffin colors, c. 1960s.

Indiana Glass. Sandwich pieces reproduced by Indiana Glass. Indiana also produced this line in a blue color.

White Lace

The Glassport factory produced White Lace, #741, from the Sandwich molds, in the Milk Glass color. White Lace was offered in twenty items from 1957-1963.

1957 White Lace pamphlet.

White Lace. Milk Glass 741-80, 11 1/2" Footed Cake Salver. $55-75.

White Lace. Milk Glass:
#741-121, 4" h. One-Lite Candlesticks. $30-45 pair.
#741-41, 10" Salad Bowl. $30-45.

1957 White Lace pamphlet.

White Lace. Milk Glass #741-45, 3-Piece Mayo Set: Plate 7", Bowl 4 3/4". $35-55.

White Lace. Milk Glass #741-78, 18" Footed Fruit Basket. $35-55.

Gold Lace

The #741 Gold Lace line is seldom seen today. Gold Lace was produced from the Sandwich molds in the same twenty items as White Lace. Gold highlights were added to the embossed area of the pattern. Gold Lace was made c. 1959-1961, with production at the Glassport factory.

 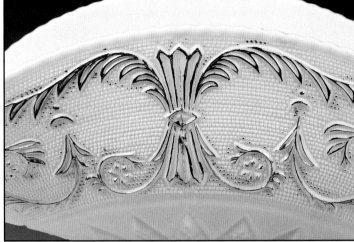

Gold Lace. Milk Glass #741-78, 18" Footed Fruit Basket. $45-65.   Detail of Gold Lace decoration.

Tear Drop

The #301 Tear Drop pattern was a very successful reproduction for Tiffin Glass. Tear Drop was produced in Crystal, c. 1957-1963, in about eighty items, including a full line of stemware. The Smoke color was added in 1959 in twenty items, and was made through 1963. Around 1960, the Flame color was used to produce seven items. There was no production of Tear Drop after 1963. All production of Tear Drop took place at the Tiffin Factory.

Tear Drop. Crystal:
  #301-123, 10" h. 2-Lite Candelabra with Prisms. $100-125 pair.
  #301-121, 4" h. 1-Lite Candlestick. $25-45 pair.

Tear Drop. Smoke:
  #301-34, 11" 2-Handled Plate. $15-25.
  #301, 8 oz. Cream. $10-15.

Tear Drop. Flame:
  #301-106, 11 1/2" Crimped Flower Bowl. $45-65.
  #301-29, 7" 4-Handled Plate. $20-30.
  #301-50, 9" 3-Handled Relish. $35-50.
  #301-90, 6" 4-Handled Bon Bon. $20-30.
   Note the difference in intensity of color between the pieces. Produced c. 1960.

Murano

The Murano, #127 line, was reproduced in several sizes and colors by Tiffin Glass. Murano can be easily distinguished by the open work on the rim. The bowls and vases can be found in Crystal, Dawn, Citron Green, Copen Blue, Flame, Golden Banana, Plum, Tiffin Rose, and Desert Red. The candlesticks are limited to the colors of Crystal, Golden Banana, Plum and Tiffin Rose.

Murano.
Flame #127-108, 10" Crimped Bowl. $100-125.
Copen Blue #127-113, 7" h. Flared Vase. $75-100.

Murano. Golden Banana:
#127-122, 4 7/8" One-Lite Candlesticks. $90-110 pair.
#127-107, 11 1/2" Center Bowl. $75-100.

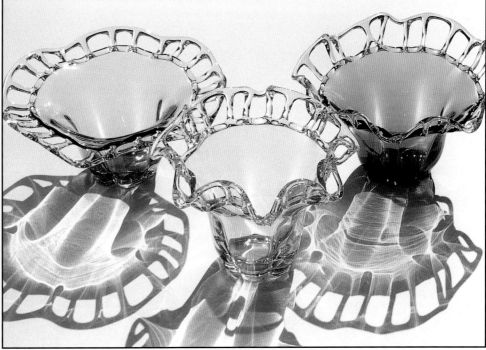

Murano. Clockwise from lower left:
Golden Banana #127-121, 4 7/8" One-Lite Candlestick. $45-60.
Plum #127-122, 4 7/8" One-Lite Candlestick. $45-60.
Tiffin Rose #127-121, 4 7/8" One-Lite Candlestick. $50-70.
Golden Banana #127-121, 4 7/8" One-Lite Candlestick. $45-60.
Plum #127-121, 4 7/8" One-Lite Candlestick. $45-60.

Murano.
Tiffin Rose #127-108, 10" Crimped Bowl. $125-150.
Dawn #9127-133, 7" h. Flared Vase. $125-150.
Desert Red #127-108, 10" Crimped Bowl. $45-65.

Kimberly and Hilton

The #22 ruby stained Kimberly, and the #22 blue stained Hilton lines utilize the same original Duncan and Miller blanks. The color of the stain determines the line name. Kimberly and Hilton were first reproduced by the United States Glass Company in 1957. Kimberly and Hilton were still offered in 1960 in ruby and blue stain. In addition, the #22 line was also available with Platinum or Gold trim in 1960.

Kimberly. Crystal with ruby stain #22-1, 8 1/2" oz. Goblets. $10-15 each.

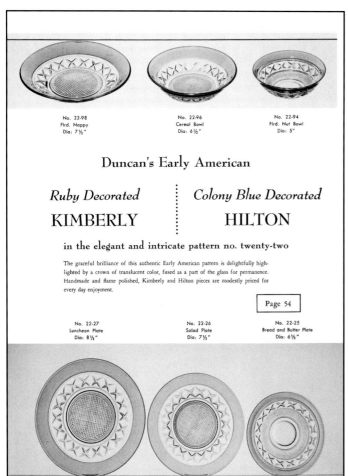

No. 22-98 Flrd. Nappy Dia: 7½" No. 22-96 Cereal Bowl Dia: 6½" No. 22-94 Flrd. Nut Bowl Dia: 5"

Duncan's Early American

Ruby Decorated | *Colony Blue Decorated*
KIMBERLY | HILTON

in the elegant and intricate pattern no. twenty-two

The graceful brilliance of this authentic Early American pattern is delightfully high-lighted by a crown of translucent color, fused as a part of the glass for permanence. Handmade and flame polished, Kimberly and Hilton pieces are modestly priced for every day enjoyment.

Page 54

No. 22-27 Luncheon Plate Dia: 8½" No. 22-26 Salad Plate Dia: 7½" No. 22-25 Bread and Butter Plate Dia: 6½"

1957 United States Glass Company #93 catalog page.

No. 22-10 6 oz. Sundae Height: 4" No. 22-1 8½ oz. Goblet Height: 5½" No. 22-3 3 oz. Cocktail Height: 3½" No. 22-4 3 oz. Wine Height: 3¾" No. 22-8 1 oz. Cordial Height: 3¼"

No. 22-11 12 oz. Ice Tea Height: 5¼" No. 22-12 10 oz. Water Tumbler Height: 4¼" No. 22-13 5½ oz. Juice Height: 3½"

No. 22-44 Mayonnaise Dia: 4½"
No. 22-45 3 pc. Mayonnaise Set

Page 55

No. 22-99 Crpd. Indiv. Chip Bowl No. 22-97 Crimped Nut Dish Dia: 6½" No. 22-95 Crimped Nappy Dia: 5¼"

1957 United States Glass Company #93 catalog page.

Contour

Duncan and Miller's #153 Contour line had limited reproduction by Tiffin Glass. Three sizes of flower bowls and the large crimped vase were only produced in the Dawn color. The two Contour molds that were used most often were the tulip ash tray and the block candlestick, which were made in: Desert Red, Dawn, Crystal, Citron Green, Copen Blue, Black, Smoke, and Greenbriar. When the block candlestick is placed inside the tulip ash tray, it is called a candlelight garden set.

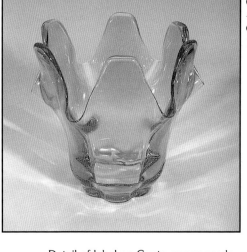

Contour. Dawn #9153-114, 8" h. Crimped Vase. $150-175.

Contour. Top to Bottom:
Dawn #9153-108, 10 1/2" Flower Bowl. $110-135.
Dawn #9153-106, 8" Miniature Flower Bowl. $90-115.
Dawn #9153-110, 6 1/2" Candlelight Garden Set. $75-100.
Copen Blue #153-98, 6 1/2" Tulip Ash Tray. $35-50.
Copen Blue #153-121, 2" h. Block Candlestick. $20-30.

Detail of label on Contour vase reads: "Handmade Duncan, Dichroic Dawn." Dichroic means having two colors. The Dawn color (lavender) changes to a light blue color under fluorescent lighting. This is a U.S. Glass label, not an original Duncan and Miller Glass Company label. This label is seldom seen, and it was used on items produced in the Dawn color from the Duncan and Miller Division of the United States Glass Company.

Contour. Greenbriar:
#153-110, 6 3/4" Candlelight Garden Set. $25-40 set.
#153-121, 2" Block Candlestick. $10-15.

Contour. Smoke #153-110, 6 3/4" Candlelight Garden Sets. $25-45 set.

Contour. Copen Blue #153-110, 6 1/2" Candlelight Garden Set. The #153-121 Block Candlestick inserted into the #153-98 Tulip Ash Tray comprises the Candlelight Garden Set. $65-85.

Contour. Black with satin finish:
#153-98, 6 1/2" Tulip Ash Tray. $25-45.
#153-121, 2" h. Block Candlestick. $15-25.

Homestead

The Homestead #563 design was a very early Duncan and Miller pattern. In 1957, Tiffin Glass reproduced the punch bowl in Crystal and five items in Milk Glass: handled nappy, nappy, footed compote, bowl, and 6" vase. These items were produced at the Glassport factory. Three items were offered in the Plum, Golden Banana, Cobalt Blue, and Empire Green colors: the footed compote, bowl, and vase. In 1962, two additional items were offered in Plum and Golden Banana: a 13" plate, and a cake salver. Items found in Empire Green would be considered scarce.

Homestead.
Cobalt Blue #563-5, 6" h. Vase. $90-110.
Milk Glass #763-5, 6" h. Vase. $20-30.

Homestead. Milk Glass:
#763-5, 6" h. Vase. $20-30.
#763-1, 8 1/2" h. Footed Compote. $45-65.
#763-4, 5" Handled Nappy. $15-20.
#763-2, 9" Bowl. $30-45.

Homestead.
Plum #563-1, 8 1/2" h. Footed Compote. $90-110.
Cobalt Blue #563-1, 8 1/2" h. Footed Compote. $150-175.
Milk Glass #763-1, 8 1/2" h. Footed Compote. $45-65.
Golden Banana #563-1, 8 1/2" h. Footed Compote. $90-110.
When an item was produced in the Milk Glass color, the first number of the line number was replaced with the number 7.

Detail of Homestead pattern.

Homestead.
  Golden Banana #563-2, 9" Bowl. $55-75.
  Golden Banana #563-5, 6" h. Vase. $35-50.
  Plum #563-1, 8 1/2" h. Footed Compote. $90-110. The bowl of
    the compote has been worked to a vase-like shape. This was
    not a production item.
  Plum #563-5, 6" h. Vase. $35-50.

Homestead.
  Plum #563-6, 13" Plate. $25-45.
  Golden Banana #563-7, 12" Cake Salver. $75-100.

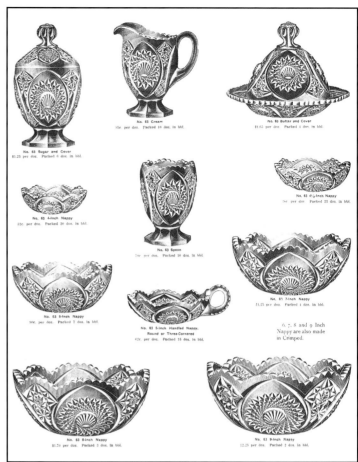

Duncan and Miller Glass Company catalog page.

Duncan and Miller Glass Company catalog page.

Duncan and Miller Glass Company catalog page.

Hobnail

Duncan and Miller's #118 Hobnail pattern saw considerable reproduction by Tiffin Glass. The only documented item produced in Crystal is the cake salver. At least seventeen items were made in Milk Glass at Glassport, in 1957. In 1961 and 1962, there was limited production in the colors of Plum, Golden Banana, Cobalt Blue, Empire Green, and Tiffin Rose at the Tiffin factory. The Empire Green color is the hardest color to locate in the Hobnail line.

Hobnail. Crystal 118-80, 10"
Footed Salver. $65-85.

Hobnail.
Golden Banana #518-25, 4 1/2" Candlestick. $25-40.
Plum #518-25, 4 1/2" Candlestick. $25-40.
Tiffin Rose #518-25, 4 1/2" Candlestick. $40-60.
Milk Glass #718-25, 4 1/2" Candlestick. $15-20.
Cobalt Blue #518-25, 4 1/2" Candlestick. $40-60.

Hobnail.
 Plum #518-29, 6 1/2" h. Rose Bowl. $40-60.
 Milk Glass #718-18, 6 1/2" h. Footed Compote. $25-35.
 Plum #518-18, 6 1/2" h. Footed Compote. $40-60.
 Golden Banana #518-29, 6 1/2" h. Rose Bowl. $40-60.

Hobnail. Plum:
 #518-25, 4 1/2" Candlesticks. $55-75 pair.
 #518-27, 11 1/2" Crimped Bowl. $55-75.

Hobnail.
 Golden Banana #518-20, 9 1/2", 2-Handled Bowl. $45-65.
 Golden Banana #518-3, Saucer Champagne. $10-15.
 Plum #518-1, Goblet. $15-20.
 Tiffin Rose #518-1, Goblet. $10-20.
  A #518-2, Footed Tumbler and #518-4, Cocktail were also produced.

Hobnail. Tiffin Rose:
  #518, 10" h. Tall Handled Basket. $65-85.
  #518, 4 1/4" Top Hat. $30-45.
  #518, 7 1/2" h. Footed Crimped Compote. $55-75.
  #518, 6" Handled Bon Bon. $30-45.
  #518, 8 1/2" Deep Nappy. $55-75.
  #518, 5" h. Oval Vase. $35-50.
  #518-17, 12" Flower Floater. $30-45.
  #518, 7 1/2" h. Footed Compote. $55-75.

Hobnail.
  Tiffin Rose #518-15, 11 1/2"
    Basket. $100-125.
  Golden Banana #518-15, 11 1/2"
    Basket. $75-100.
    Also produced in Plum.

Provincial

The Provincial #75 line was reproduced at Glassport c. 1959 from Duncan and Miller's Diamond pattern. This is the one instance where the United States Glass Company changed the original manufacturer's name from the Duncan and Miller lines. The United States Glass Company usually kept the original Duncan and Miller name to capitalize on the name awareness already present. Provincial consisted of about twenty-seven items in Crystal. The stemware and tableware were also offered in Crystal with ruby stain. In 1960, seventeen items were offered with gold or platinum trim. After 1960, Provincial was no longer listed, due to low sales volume.

1959 United States Glass Company photograph showing items available in Crystal for the Provincial pattern.

1959 United States Glass Company promotional photograph for the Provincial pattern. Crystal with ruby stain:
  #75-7, Seafood Cocktail. $5-10.
  #75-2, Saucer Champagne. $5-10.
  #75-1, Goblet. $10-15.
  #75-5, Footed Ice Tea. $10-15.
  #75-6, Footed Juice $5-10.

Swirl

A few items were reproduced from Duncan and Miller's #121 Swirl line. The #121-117 cornucopia was produced in Crystal and Dawn, in the mid 1950s. In 1962, the #562-10 vase, the #562-15 crimped vase, and the #562-11 center bowl were produced in Plum, Golden Banana, and Tiffin Rose. Production took place at the Tiffin factory.

Swirl.
    Tiffin Rose #562-15, 8" h.
    Crimped Vase. $85-110.
    Golden Banana #562-10, 8" h.
    Vase. $65-85.

Swirl.
    Tiffin Rose #562-11, 13" Center Bowl.
    $85-110.
    Plum #562-11, 13" Center Bowl. $65-85.
    Golden Banana #562-11, 13" Center
    Bowl. $65-85.

Swirl. Dawn #9121-117, 14"
Cornucopia. $110-135.

Georgian

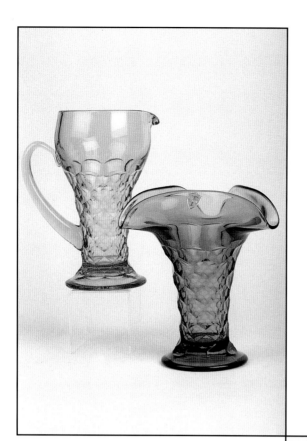

The Georgian #564 pattern was introduced in January, 1962 in three colors: Plum, Golden Banana, and Tiffin Rose. This line was reproduced using Duncan and Miller molds. The large vase mold from Duncan and Miller was reworked to form the cupped and flared jugs. Approximately eighteen items can be found in Tiffin's Georgian line. Production at the Tiffin factory was very limited, with about a two-year run.

Tiffin Rose #564-4, 8" h. Cupped Jug.
  $65-85.
Plum #564-6, 7 3/4" h. Flower Arranger.
  $55-75.

Georgian. Plum:
  #564-7, Juice Tumbler. $5-10.
  #564-5, 8" h. Flared Jug. $45-65.
  #564-6, 7" Flower Arranger. $55-75.
  #564-14, 13 1/2" Flower Floater. $35-55.

Georgian.
  Tiffin Rose #564-2, 8 1/4" Flower Arranger.
    $65-85.
  Tiffin Rose #564-3, 12" h. Basket. $100-125.
  Golden Banana #564-6, 7 3/4" Flower
    Arranger. $55-75.
  Golden Banana #564-14, 13 1/2" Flower
    Floater. $35-55.
  Tiffin Rose #564-10, 5 1/2" Nut Bowl. $15-25.

Georgian.
   #564-16, Flared Mayonnaise Bowl.
   #564-17, 7" Plate.
   #15151 Ladle.

American Way

Tiffin Glass reproduced just a few items from Duncan and Miller's American Way #71 line. In the mid 1950s, the #71-121 candlestick was produced in Crystal, and the #771-1 Vase in Milk Glass at Glassport. In 1962, the #71-121 candlestick mold was used to create the #562-12 one-lite candlesticks in Crystal, Plum, Golden Banana, and Tiffin Rose at the Tiffin factory. The #71-121 was shaped after it came out of the mold, while the glass was still hot, to achieve the form of the #562-12 candlestick.

Top right: **Georgian.**
   #564-11, 8 1/2" Plate.
   #564-12, Berry Dish.

Center right: **Georgian.**
   #564-4, 8" h. Cupped Jug.
   #564-5, 8" h. Flared Jug.

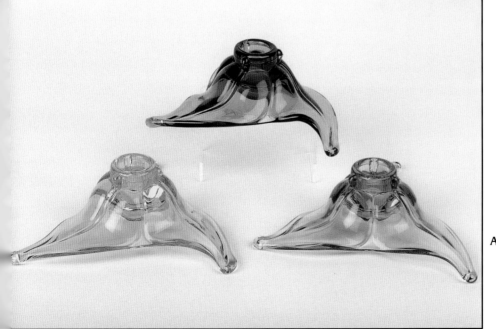

American Way.
   Golden Banana #562-12, 5 1/2" One
   Lite Candlestick. $35-50.
   Plum #562-12, 5 1/2" One Lite Candle-
   stick. $35-50.
   Tiffin Rose #562-12, 5 1/2" One Lite
   Candlestick. $40-60.

Chapter 3
Candleholders & Epergnes

Tiffin Glass reproduced many of the Duncan and Miller candleholders and epergnes in Crystal at the Glassport factory. These are in addition to the colored epergnes, which were produced at Tiffin. Other candleholders are included elsewhere under individual pattern lines.

Top left: 1959 United States Glass Company catalog page. The candleholders and epergnes shown on the 1959 catalog pages were all produced from Duncan and Miller molds. All of these have parts that screw together to create different styles. These were produced at Glassport, c. 1959-1963, and are quite difficult to find today.

Top right, bottom left, & bottom right: 1959 United States Glass Company catalog page.

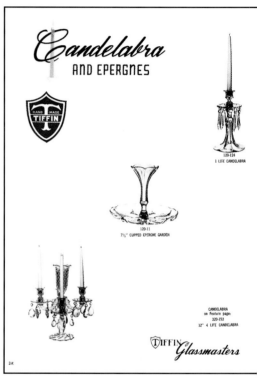

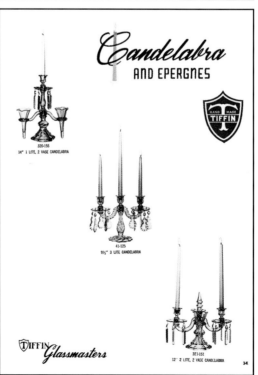

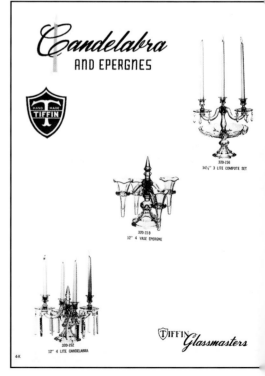

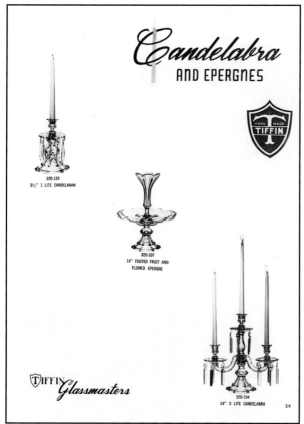

1959 United States Glass Company catalog page.

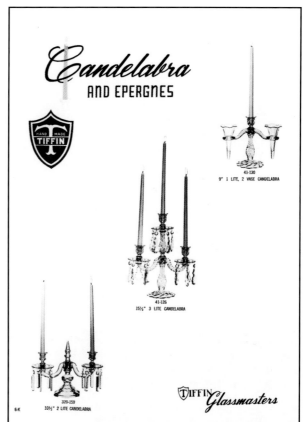

1959 United States Glass Company catalog page.

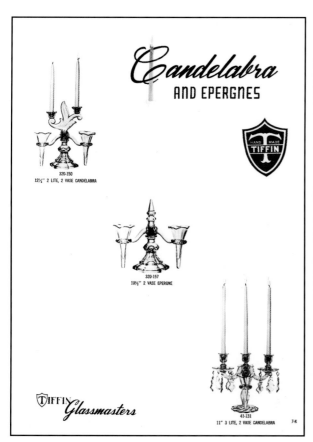

1959 United States Glass Company catalog page.

Crystal #6485-4 13 1/4" Flower Floater with
Candleholder. $35-55.

Crystal 8 3/4" 2-Lite Candlesticks, both with undocumented line numbers. The left hand candlestick is decorated with the Parkwood engraving. The undocumented candlestick on the right is similar in design and is much harder to find. $40-60. $30-50.

Crystal #5902:
7 1/2" 2-Lite Candlesticks. $75-100 pair.
10" Salad Bowl. $75-100.
All with Fuchsia etching. This style of candlestick is commonly referred to as "fan center" by collectors. Produced early 1940s.

Crystal #5904-11, 7 1/4" 2-Lite Candlestick. $25-40.
The right hand candlestick is New Martinsville's #18, shown here to compare the similarities with the Tiffin candlestick.

Crystal #5573, 3 1/2" h. Candle Holders, c. 1955. Also produced in Black. $20-35 pair.

Twilight 6" h. Candleholders, undocumented line number, c. 1951. $150-175 pair.

"Aqua" #17709, 6 1/2" h. Candleholders. Made to accompany the American Manor Celestial china and crystal line. $35-55 pair.

"Aqua" with satin finish #17709, 6 1/2" Candleholders. $35-55 pair.

Golden Banana #320-
107, 14" h. Footed
Fruit and Flower
Epergne. $125-150.

Plum #320-107, 14"
h. Footed Fruit and
Flower Epergne.
$125-150. Also
produced in Empire
Green.

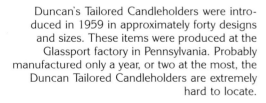

Plum #162, 9 1/4" h. Epergne Compote and Vase. $55-75.

Duncan's Tailored Candleholders were introduced in 1959 in approximately forty designs and sizes. These items were produced at the Glassport factory in Pennsylvania. Probably manufactured only a year, or two at the most, the Duncan Tailored Candleholders are extremely hard to locate.

United States Glass Company advertisement for Duncan Tailored Candleholders.

LINE NUMBER	DESCRIPTION	DOZEN	LIST
	Duncan's Tailored Candleholders (Effective January 1, 1960)		
C-1	13 1/2" tall. White with colorless glass.	52.80	4.40
C-3	9 3/4" tall. White with colorless glass.	39.60	3.30
C-4	6 1/4" tall. White with colorless glass.	33.00	2.75
C-6	12 1/2" tall. White with colorless glass.	52.80	4.40
C-7	7" tall. White with colorless glass.	33.00	2.75
C-10	6 1/4" tall. White with colorless glass.	33.00	2.75
C-12	4" tall. White with colorless glass.	26.40	2.20
C-14	5" tall. White with colorless glass.	33.00	2.75
C-15	4" tall. White with colorless glass.	26.40	2.20
C-16	5" tall. White with colorless glass.	26.40	2.20
C-19	4" tall. White with colorless glass.	26.40	2.20
C-23	12 3/4" tall. White with colorless glass.	59.40	4.95
C-26	9 1/4" tall. White with colorless glass.	33.00	2.75
C-31	10 1/4" tall. White with colorless glass.	33.00	2.75
C-32	10 1/2" tall. White or yellow with milk glass.	39.60	3.30
C-33	9 1/2" tall. White or yellow with colorless, ruby, cranberry, or blue glass.	39.60	3.30
C-34	10" tall. White or yellow with colorless glass.	39.60	3.30
C-35	10" tall. White or yellow with colorless glass.	39.60	3.30
C-36	13" tall. White or yellow with colorless glass.	39.60	3.30
C-37	13" tall. White or yellow with colorless, ruby, cranberry, or blue glass.	52.80	4.40
C-38	14" tall. White or yellow with colorless, ruby, cranberry, or blue glass.	52.80	4.40
C-39	13" tall. White or yellow with colorless glass.	52.80	4.40
C-40	15" tall. White or yellow with colorless glass.	52.80	4.40
C-41	6" tall. White or yellow with colorless, ruby, cranberry, or blue glass.	39.60	3.30
C-42	8" tall. White or yellow with colorless glass.	33.00	2.75
C-43	10 1/2" tall. White or yellow with colorless glass.	52.80	4.40
C-44	10" tall. White or yellow with colorless glass and two epergnes.	78.00	6.50
C-45	8" tall. White or yellow with colorless glass.	33.00	2.75
C-46	9" tall. White or yellow with colorless glass.	33.00	2.75
C-47	9" tall. White or yellow with colorless glass.	33.00	2.75
C-48	13" tall. White or yellow with colorless glass.	52.80	4.40
C-49	14 1/2" tall. White or yellow with colorless glass.	52.80	4.40
C-50	14" tall. White or yellow with colorless glass.	52.80	4.40
C-51	21" tall. White or yellow with colorless glass.	66.00	5.50
C-52	8 1/2" tall. White or yellow with colorless glass.	26.40	2.20
C-53	10 1/2" tall. White or yellow with colorless glass, and eight 4" prisms.	59.40	4.95
C-54	15 1/2" tall. White or yellow with colorless glass and eight 6" prisms.	66.00	5.50
C-155	3 1/2" tall. Clear glass only.	78.00	6.50

C-33, 9 1/2" h., White or Yellow with
   colorless, ruby, cranberry, or blue glass.
C-31, 10 1/4" h., White with colorless
   glass.
C-33, 9 1/2" h., White or Yellow with
   colorless, ruby, cranberry, or blue glass.
C-33, 9 1/2" h., White or Yellow with
   colorless, ruby, cranberry, or blue glass.

C-37, 13" h., White or Yellow with
   colorless glass.
C-59, Note the use of Sandwich Glass
   molds. No other information provided.
C-1, 13 1/2" h., White with colorless
   glass.
C-23, 12 3/4" h., White with colorless
   glass.

C-47, 9" h., White or Yellow with
   colorless, ruby, cranberry, or blue
   glass.
C-53, 10 1/2" h., White or Yellow with
   colorless glass, and eight 4" prisms.
C-32, 10 1/2" h., White or Yellow with
   milk glass.
C-64, no other information provided.

C-33, 9 1/2" h., White or Yellow with colorless, ruby, cranberry, or blue glass.
C-33, 9 1/2" h., White or Yellow with colorless, ruby cranberry, or blue glass.
C-45, 8" h., White or Yellow with colorless glass.

C-41, 6" h., White or Yellow with colorless, ruby, cranberry, or blue glass.
C-4, 6 1/4" h., White with colorless glass.
C-14, 6" h., White with colorless glass.

C-6, 12 1/2" h., White with colorless glass.
C-38, 14" h., White or Yellow with colorless, ruby, cranberry, or blue glass.
C-65, No other information provided.
C-12, 13" h., White or Yellow with colorless glass.

C-39, 13" h., White or Yellow with
  colorless glass.
C-54, 15 1/2" h., White or Yellow with
  colorless glass and eight 6" prisms.
C-50, 14" h., White or Yellow with
  colorless glass.

C-42, 8" h., White or Yellow with
  colorless glass. (This candlestick
  utilized the #10 candlestick.)
C-52, 8 1/2" h., White or Yellow with
  colorless glass.

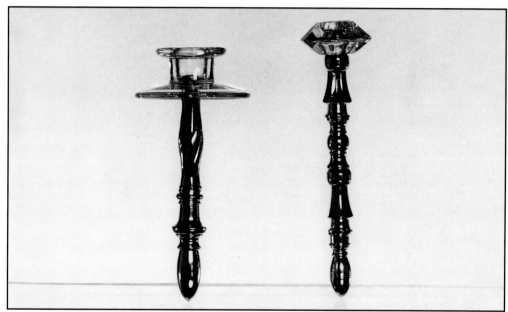

C-10, 6 1/4" h., White or Yellow with
  colorless glass.
C-46, 9" h., White or Yellow with
  colorless glass.
C-7, 7" h., White with colorless glass.

C-155, 3 1/2" h., Clear glass only.
C-15, 4" h., White with colorless glass.
C-19, 4" h., White with colorless glass.
C-16, 5" h., White with colorless glass.

C-36, 13" h., White or Yellow with colorless glass.
C-40, 15" h., White or Yellow with colorless glass.
C-49, 14 1/2" h., White or Yellow with colorless glass.
C-48, 13" h., White or Yellow with colorless glass.

C-51, 21" h., White or Yellow with colorless glass.
C-67, No other information provided. (Note the use of a Williamsburg mold for the base.)

Chapter 4
Ash Trays

The majority of the pressed ash trays manufactured by Tiffin Glass were produced from Duncan and Miller molds. The ash trays were available in a variety of colors, and a number of sizes. Some of the lines also offered a covered cigarette box.

1967 Smoking Accessories by Tiffin.

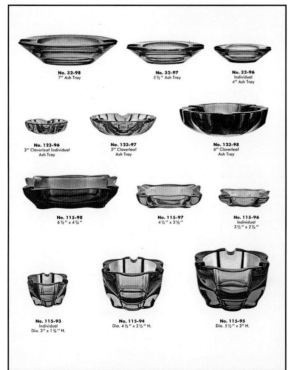

Pall Mall. Crystal:

#30-98, 6 1/2" Rectangular Ash Tray. The etching on the ash tray reads: "National Machinery 1874-1974." National Machinery is a Tiffin, Ohio, factory still in operation. In 1974, the company gave every employee this crystal ash tray in a cloth bag, along with a $100 bill to commemorate the factory's 100th year of operation. $15-25.

#30-99, 8" Rectangular Ash Tray with unidentified engraving. $25-35.

#30-98, 6 1/2" Rectangular Ash Tray with color-filled etching of a polo scene. $25-35.

   The rectangular ash trays are part of the Pall Mall line and were produced from a Duncan and Miller Glass Company mold.

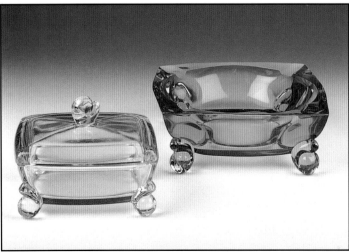

Clover Leaf. Left to right, top to bottom:

   Beige Opal #123-97, 5" Clover Leaf Ash Tray. $15-25.
   Milk Glass #123-97, 5" Clover Leaf Ash Tray. $10-15.
   Plum #123-98, 6" Clover Leaf Ash Tray. $20-30.
   Dawn #9123-98, 6" Clover Leaf Ash Tray. $35-50.
   Tiffin Rose #123-98, 6" Clover Leaf Ash Tray. $35-50.
   Golden Banana #123-97, 5" Clover Leaf Ash Tray. $15-25.
   Copen Blue #123-96, 3" Clover Leaf Ash Tray. $10-15.
   Plum #123-97, 5" Clover Leaf Ash Tray. $15-25.
    There are three sizes of Clover Leaf ash trays: 3", 5", and 6". These were produced from Duncan and Miller Glass Company molds.

Patio.

   Dawn #9152-99, 5" Cigarette Box and cover. $65-85.
   Copen Blue #152-98, 5 1/2" Ash Tray. $20-30.
    The Patio ash trays were produced from a Duncan and Miller Glass Company mold.

Cobalt Blue #115-97, 4 1/2" Rectangular Ash Trays. Produced from Duncan and Miller molds. $25-45 each.

Copen Blue # 32-97, 5 1/2" Oval Ash Trays. $20-30, $10-15.

Top ash tray is embossed with the Tiffin shield and the words, "Tiffin Glass Festival." A limited number of these souvenir ash trays were produced in Crystal and Copen Blue for a Tiffin Glass Festival held in downtown Tiffin, Ohio, in 1965.

Pine 9 3/8" Square Ash Tray produced as a special order and embossed "Anderson Loan Association, Founded 1888." $30-50.

Crystal with cranberry stain, #5804, 8 1/2" 6-piece Smart Set. Also decorated with ruby, amber, amethyst, and gold stain. This photo shows the Smart Set with the center placed cigarette box, and the four ash trays stacked in the side compartments. Produced mid to late 1950s. $35-55.

#5804 Smart Set with all six pieces displayed.

Chapter 5
Punch Sets

Punch sets were always a part of the United States Glass Company's price lists, until bankruptcy in 1962. After 1963, punch sets were no longer offered. One probable reason is that all the punch sets were produced at Glassport, and the Glassport factory was destroyed by a tornado in August, 1963. Some of the punch sets, such as Moon and Stars, Bullseye, Pin Wheel and Star, and Williamsburg were early U.S. Glass lines. When the United States Glass Company acquired the Duncan and Miller molds in 1955, several Duncan and Miller punch sets became part of the U.S. Glass inventory, yet retained their original names. In addition to the King's Crown pattern, Moon and Stars, Bullseye and Williamsburg were also offered with ruby stain. The Moon and Stars punch set was also available in Milk Glass in 1952.

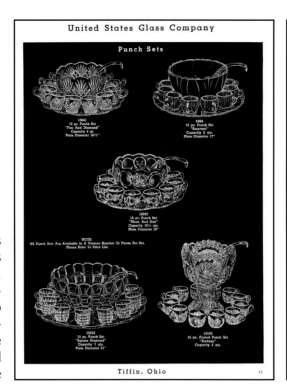

1956 United States Glass Company catalog page.
#15041 Fan and Diamond. $150-175 set.
#5804 Smart Set. $75-100 set.
#15093 Moon and Star. $150-175 set.
#15025 Square Diamond. $150-175 set.
#15150 Antique. $150-175 set.

1959 United States Glass Company catalog page
#111 Pin Wheel and Star. Pin Wheel and Star was renamed Regal in 1963, and was available with with a metal base in a gold, silver, or antiqued gold finish. The Pin Wheel and Star punch bowl has been reproduced by Indiana Glass. 15 pc. set. $150-175.

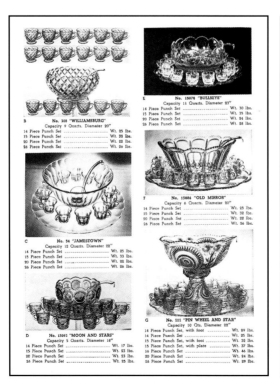

1959 United States Glass Company catalog page.
#308 Williamsburg. $100-125.
#54 Jamestown. $100-125.
#15093 Moon and Stars. $150-175.
#15078 Bullseye. $150-175.
#15086 Old Mirror. $100-125.
#111 Pin Wheel and Star. $200-225.
Prices are for 15-piece sets.

1959 United States Glass Company catalog page.
334 Colonial. $100-125.
#15041 Fan and Diamond. $150-175.
#58 Royal. $100-125.
#308 Williamsburg. $100-125.
#40 Saratoga. $150-175.
#15025 Square Diamond. $150-175.
Prices are for 15-piece sets.

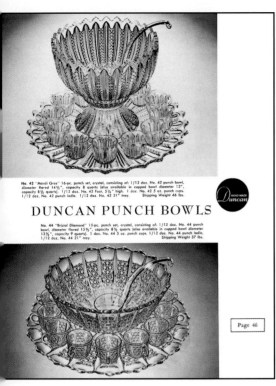

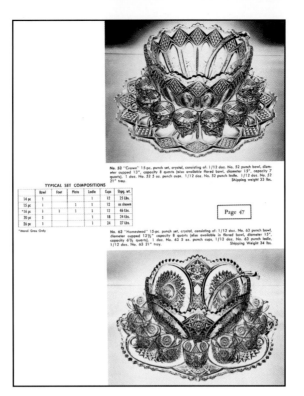

No. 42 "Mardi Gras" 16-pc. punch set, crystal, consisting of: 1/12 doz. No. 42 punch bowl, diameter flared 14½", capacity 8 quarts (also available in cupped bowl diameter 13", capacity 8½ quarts), 1/12 doz. No. 42 Foot, 5½" high. 1 doz. No. 42 5 oz. punch cups. 1/12 doz. No. 42 punch ladle. 1/12 doz. No. 42 21" tray. Shipping Weight 46 lbs.

DUNCAN PUNCH BOWLS

No. 44 "Bristol Diamond" 15-pc. punch set, crystal, consisting of: 1/12 doz. No. 44 punch bowl, diameter flared 15½", capacity 8½ quarts (also available in cupped bowl diameter 13½", capacity 9 quarts). 1/12 doz. No. 44 5 oz. punch cups. 1/12 doz. No. 44 punch ladle. 1/12 doz. No. 44 21" tray. Shipping Weight 37 lbs.

No. 52 "Crown" 15-pc. punch set, crystal, consisting of: 1/12 doz. No. 52 punch bowl, diameter cupped 13", capacity 8 quarts (also available flared bowl, diameter 13", capacity 7 quarts). 1 doz. No. 52 5 oz. punch cups. 1/12 doz. No. 52 punch ladle. 1/12 doz. No. 52 tray. Shipping weight 33 lbs.

TYPICAL SET COMPOSITIONS

	Bowl	Foot	Plate	Ladle	Cups	Shpg. wt.
14 pc	1			1	12	25 Lbs.
15 pc	1			1	12	as shown
*16 pc	1	1		1	12	46 Lbs.
20 pc	1			1	18	24 Lbs.
26 pc	1			1	24	27 Lbs.

*Mardi Gras Only

No. 63 "Homestead" 15-pc. punch set, crystal, consisting of: 1/12 doz. No. 63 punch bowl, diameter cupped 12½", capacity 8 quarts (also available in flared bowl, diameter 13", capacity 6½ quarts). 1 doz. No. 63 5 oz. punch cups. 1/12 doz. No. 63 punch ladle. 1/12 doz. No. 63 tray. Shipping Weight 34 lbs.

Page 46

Page 47

1957 United States Glass Company #93 catalog page.
> #42 Mardi Gras. $200-225 set.
> #44 Bristol Diamond. $150-175 set.

1957 United States Glass Company #93 catalog page.
> #52 Crown. $150-175 set.
> #63 Homestead. $150-175 set.

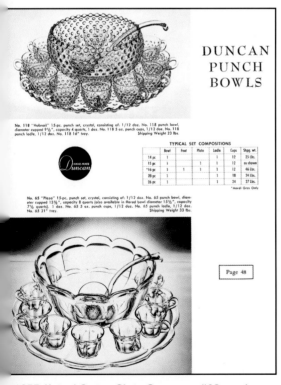

DUNCAN PUNCH BOWLS

No. 118 "Hobnail" 15-pc. punch set, crystal, consisting of: 1/12 doz. No. 118 punch bowl, diameter cupped 9½", capacity 4 quarts. 1 doz. No. 118 5 oz. punch cups. 1/12 doz. No. 118 punch ladle. 1/12 doz. No. 118 16" tray. Shipping Weight 23 lbs.

TYPICAL SET COMPOSITIONS

	Bowl	Foot	Plate	Ladle	Cups	Shpg. wt.
14 pc	1			1	12	25 Lbs.
15 pc	1			1	12	as shown
*16 pc	1	1	1	1	12	46 Lbs.
20 pc	1			1	18	24 Lbs.
26 pc	1			1	24	27 Lbs.

*Mardi Gras Only

No. 65 "Plaza" 15-pc. punch set, crystal, consisting of: 1/12 doz. No. 65 punch bowl, diameter cupped 13½", capacity 8 quarts (also available in flared bowl diameter 15½", capacity 7½ quarts). 1 doz. No. 65 5 oz. punch cups. 1/12 doz. No. 65 punch ladle. 1/12 doz. No. 65 21" tray.

Page 48

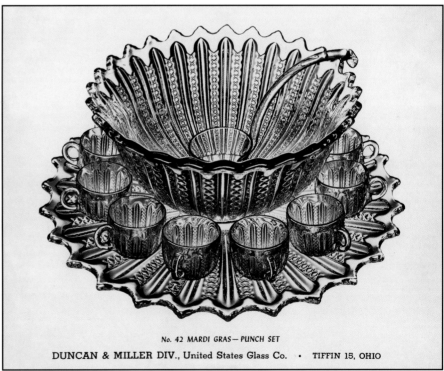

No. 42 MARDI GRAS — PUNCH SET

DUNCAN & MILLER DIV., United States Glass Co. • TIFFIN 15, OHIO

1957 United States Glass Company #93 catalog page.
> #118 Hobnail. $150-175 set.
> #65 Plaza. $100-125 set.

#42 Mardi Gras. $150-175 set.

#15061 Rattan.
Rattan was known as Tempo in the 1920s and 1930s. $100-125 set.

Crystal #4016 King's Crown, cupped. $250-300 set.
Crystal with ruby stain #4016 King's Crown, cupped. $600-650 set.

Crystal #4016 King's Crown, flared. $250-300 set.
Crystal with ruby stain, #4016 King's Crown, flared. $600-650 set.

#54 Jamestown, Crystal with allover gold decoration. $250-300 set.

Milk Glass #7041 Fan and Diamond. $175-200 set.

Chapter 6
Decorative Jars

Decorative/Apothecary jars have a long history with the United States Glass Company. Store, confection, and apothecary jars are pictured in many U.S. Glass catalogs dating from the late 1890s to 1960. The majority of these jars were produced at Factory F (Ripley and Company), located in Pittsburgh. In the 1950s U.S. Glass started to market the jars as Decorative Jars, to be used to store candy, condiments, soap, pasta, etc. The jars became very popular and remain so today; these were produced at Glassport, with or without ground stoppers. Decorative jars remained in the catalog listings until 1963, when they were discontinued.

1959 United States Glass Company catalog page.

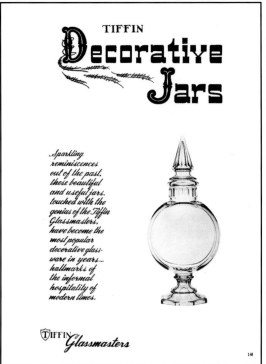

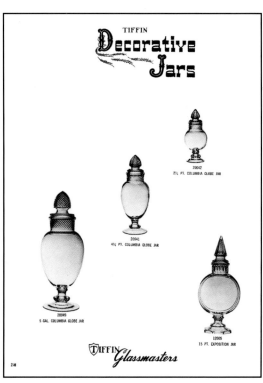

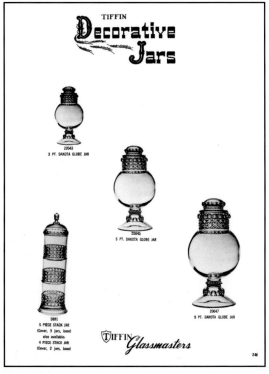

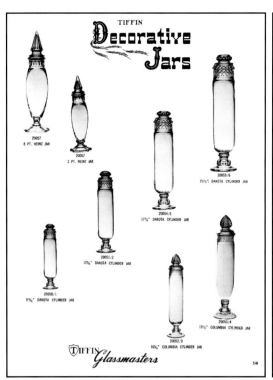

1959 United States Glass Company catalog page.

1959 United States Glass Company catalog page.

The L.E. Smith Glass Company of Mount Pleasant, Pennsylvania reproduced three sizes of the Dakota cylinder jar. These have a yellowish cast, while the United States Glass Company jars are crystal clear.

1959 United States Glass Company catalog page.

1926 United States Glass Company catalog page featuring jars made at Factory F, Ripley & Company, located in Pittsburgh, Pennsylvania, and Factory U, located at Gas City, Indiana.

#5891 5-Piece Stack Jar disassembled showing the base, cover, and three jars.

Crystal with ruby stain #5891, 18" h., 5-Piece Stack Jar. $425-500. Each jar is lightly embossed 'Patented May 20, 1873.'

Milk Glass #791 4-Piece Stack Jar. $300-325. These retailed for $7.15 in 1960. A 5-Piece Stack Jar in Milk Glass was also produced.

Early 1940s United States Glass Company catalog page.

Early 1940s United States Glass Company catalog page.

1958 United States Glass Company promotional photograph.
#20040, 1 1/2" lb. Jar, decorated "Tea."
#20040, 2 lb. Jar, decorated "Coffee."
#20040, 3 1/2" lb. Jar, decorated "Sugar."
#20058, 5 lb. Jar, decorated "Flour."
These were available with White, Black, Yellow, Red, or Blue decoration.

#20057, 15 1/2" h., 2 pt. Heinz Jar; Crystal with allover gold decoration. $150-175.
#20044, 12 1/4" h., 5 pt. Egyptian Jar, unknown decoration. $150-175.
#20053/4, 19 1/2" h., Columbia Cylinder Jar, produced c. 1956, unknown decoration. $150-175.

Milk Glass #791, 9 1/2" h., 3-Piece Stack Jar. $250-275

Chapter 7
Hospitality Line

The Hospitality Line, introduced in 1958, consisted of glass items with metal/mesh holders. The United States Glass Company paired existing items in their inventory with metal and gave them a new look, creating a new sales item. The glass items were produced at the Glassport factory; the metal holders were purchased from an outside company. This line was offered for a very brief period of time.

#9 Condiment Caddy, introduced c. 1958. $55-75 set.

UNITED STATES GLASS COMPANY
TIFFIN, OHIO

PRESENTS

The Hospitality Line

An Item For Every Room In The Home
Also Group Of Party Servers

No. 1 Beauty Bar

No. 2 Priscillas Pantry

No. 3 Spice Shelf

No. 4 Cruet Set

No. 5 Hanging Apothecary Jar

No. 6 Ice Bucket

No. 7 Rose Epergne

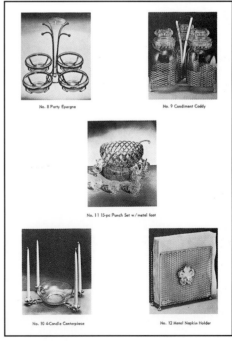

No. 8 Party Epergne

No. 9 Condiment Caddy

No. 11 15-pc Punch Set w/metal foot

No. 10 4-Candle Centerpiece

No. 12 Metal Napkin Holder

1958 United States Glass Company catalog page.

1958 United States Glass Company catalog page.

1958 United States Glass Company catalog page.

Chapter 8
Casual Crystal

Advertised as Franciscan Casual Crystal in 1974, Madeira and Cabaret were produced to coordinate with the Franciscan China produced by the Interpace Corporation. In the 1970s informal dining was in vogue and heavy, thick-walled crystal and stoneware produced in earth tone colors replaced the finer lead crystal stemware and china table settings. The popularity of Madeira and Cabaret continued until the closing of the Tiffin factory in 1980.

Top: **Madeira.**
Smoke #120-1, 9 oz. Goblet. $3-8.
Rose #120-11, 10 oz. Double Old Fashion. $5-10.
Smoke #120-34/35, Ice Tub with Lid. $15-25.
Olive #120-2, 6 oz. Sherbet, flared top. $5-10.
Rose #120-2, 6 oz. Sherbet. $5-10.
Smoke #120-6, 6 oz. Juice/Wine, crimped top. $3-8.
Blue #120-12, 14 oz. Hi-Ball/Tumbler. $5-10.

Center: **Madeira.**
Smoke #120-1, 9 oz. Goblet. $3-8.
Cornsilk #120-1, 9 oz. Goblet. $5-10.
Rancho Ruby #120-1, 9 oz. Goblet. $5-10.
Rose #120-1, 9 oz. Goblet. $5-10.
Twilight #120-1, 9 oz. Goblet. $10-15.
"Green Opalescent" #120-1, 9 oz. Goblet. $10-15.
Persimmon #120-3, 12 oz. Iced Tea. $5-10.
Apple Green #120-3, 12 oz. Iced Tea. $5-10.
Blue #120-3, 12 oz. Iced Tea, crimped top. $5-10.

Bottom: **Madeira.** Smoke:
#120-7, Double Old Fashions. $3-8 each.
#120-33, One Quart Carafe. $10-15.

Madeira

The Madeira #120 line was introduced in January, 1971 in five colors: Blue, Citron, Olive, Smoke, and Ice (Crystal). Items offered were: a goblet, sherbet, juice/wine, ice tea, hiball/tumbler, and double old fashion. The Plum, Cornsilk (yellow) and Rancho Ruby colors were added in 1972, along with three additional items: a handled mug, carafe, an ice bucket with cover. The mug, carafe, and ice bucket were only available in the Rancho Ruby, Smoke, and Olive colors. Colors added in later years were Clover (green) Pumpkin (Desert Red), Pearl, and Rose. There were some additional colors that were made for which we have no documentation: Twilight, Milk Glass, "Green Opalescent," and "Blue Opalescent." The Madeira line was an extremely good seller for Tiffin, and remained in production through 1980. When Madeira was first introduced in 1971, the Lancaster Glass Corporation was contracted to produce the goblet and ice tea in the Blue, Citron, Olive, and Smoke colors. The other items at that time were produced at the Tiffin factory. It is unknown how long Lancaster produced items for Tiffin. It has also been reported that some production of the Rancho Ruby color took place in Mexico.

Cabaret

Introduced in 1974 as line #121, Cabaret was produced in four stemware sizes: a 9 oz. goblet, 6 oz. sherbet, a 12 oz. iced tea, a 6 oz. juice/wine. A 7" bowl was produced through 1976. Cabaret was offered in the colors of Apple Green, Cobalt Blue, Cornsilk, and Pink, with Persimmon (Desert Red) added in 1975. This line was discontinued in early 1979.

Madeira.
Olive #120-32, 14 oz. Mug. $10-15. "Grey" 14" h. Bud Vase. Not a production item. $15-20.

The left and middle items are reproductions of the Madeira and Cabaret lines, made by the Mosser Glass Company of Cambridge, Ohio. The crimped iced tea has an embossed M on the base. The right item is the Cabaret iced tea, shown for comparison purposes.

Cabaret. Persimmon, Apple Green #121-10, 7" Bowls. $10-15 each.

Cabaret.
Cornsilk #121-01, 9 oz. Goblet. $5-10. Cobalt Blue #121-03, 12 oz. Iced Tea. $10-15. Pink #121-06, 6 oz. Juice/Wine. $5-10. Apple Green #121-03, 12 oz. Ice Tea. $5-10. Blue #121-01, 9 oz. Goblet. $5-10. Pink #121-03, 12 oz. Iced Tea. $5-10. Persimmon #121-06, 6 oz. Juice/Wine. $5-10. A #121-02, 6 oz. Sherbet was also produced.

Chapter 9
Miscellaneous Pressed Ware

Tiffin's diverse production included many items that were not covered by a pattern name. These items served a variety of uses: vases, bowls, dispensers, etc. Several old U.S. Glass and Duncan and Miller molds were utilized to produce Milk Glass items, which were marketed under the Duncan and Miller name.

1961 Gifts and Things pamphlet.

1959 Glass Trade Show photograph. The tables in the foreground show many different styles of punch sets. A table in the center displays many of the Duncan Tailored Candleholders. The far left shows crystal candelabra. The display on the right hand side shows an assortment of milk glass items in Sandwich, Gold Lace, Grape, Betsy Ross, and the Stack Jar. Tables in the back show items from the Empress line, and a wall of stemware in the very back of the room.

1961 Gifts and Things pamphlet.

No. 519-14
Crimped Bowl

No. 518-29
Rose Bowl

No. 509-17
Compote
Height: 6"

No. 563-2
Bowl
Dia: 9"

PLUM

PLUM

No. 518-27
Crimped Bowl
Dia: 11½"

8212
5" WEDDING BOWL

15179
4¾" HANDLED COMPOTE
AND FLOWER BLOCK

1961 Gifts and Things pamphlet.

No. 563-1
Footed Compote
Height: 8½"

308-39
1 QUART JUG

5891
5 PIECE STACK JAR
(Cover, 3 jars, base)
also available:
4 PIECE STACK JAR
(Cover, 2 jars, base)

No. 518-25
4½" Candlestick

No. 41-102
Candy Jar & Cover
Height: 8½"

GOLDEN
BANANA

15179
4¾" HANDLED COMPOTE FLOWER BLOCK

GOLDEN
BANANA

No. 519-1
Nappy
Dia: 7½"

1961 Gifts and Things pamphlet.

1961 Gifts and Things pamphlet.

1961 Gifts and Things pamphlet.

Top: Top Row, Left to Right:
  Mardi Gras #742-4, 10" h. Regular Vase. $20-35.
  Mardi Gras #742-4, 8" h. Regular Vase. $20-35.
  Hobnail #718-8, 10" Footed Cake Salver. $75-95.
  Williamsburg #708-83, 9" h. Vase. $25-45.
  Williamsburg #708-4, 7 1/2" h. Rose Bowl. $35-55.
  #750-1, 9" h. Tri-Panel Vase. $25-45.
  Hobnail #718-12, 2 qt. Jug. $45-65.
  Betsy Ross #709-16, 10" h. Vase. $30-50.
Bottom Row, Left to Right:
  Grape #719-2, 6 1/2" Nappy. $20-30.
  Grape #719-3, 5 1/2" Nappy. $15-25.
  #730-1, 9" Duck Candy Box and Cover. $30-34.
  Grape #719-5, 4 1/2" Handled Olive. $15-25.
  Grape #719-12, 1/2 lb. Butter and Cover. $65-85.
  Hobnail #718-13, 13 oz. Tumbler. $10-15.
  Grape #719-9, 7 oz. Sugar and Cover. $25-35.
  Grape #719-8, 7 oz. Cream. $25-35.
  Grape #719-13, 7 1/2" Pickle. $15-25.

Bottom: Top Row, Left to Right:
  Betsy Ross # 709-1, 52 oz. Jug. $45-65.
  Homestead # 763-1, 8 1/2" h. Compote. $45-65.
  Hobnail # 718-28, 8" h. Crimped Vase. $25-45.
  Betsy Ross # 709-12, 9 1/2" Footed Candy Box and Cover. $35-55.
  # 712-3, 12" h. Wedding Bowl and Cover. $35-55.
  # 712-2, 10" h. Wedding Bowl and Cover. $25-45.
  # 712-1, 6 1/2" h. Cigarette Box and Cover. $20-30.
  Betsy Ross # 709-3, 12 oz. Tumbler. $10-15.
Bottom Row, Left to Right:
  Betsy Ross # 709-2, 8 oz. Tumbler. $10-15.
  Williamsburg # 708-104, 8" Candy Box and Cover. $35-55.
  Betsy Ross # 709-5, 7 1/2" Three-toed Bowl. $25-40.
  Homestead # 763-4, 5" Handled Nappy. $15-20.
  Betsy Ross # 709-8, 5 oz. Sugar and Cover. $25-35.
  Betsy Ross # 709-7, 5 oz. Cream. $25-35.
  Betsy Ross # 709-13, 5 1/2" Three-toed Handled Nappy. $15-20.

Top: Top Row, Left to Right:
  Williamsburg #708-21, 8" Scalloped-edge Nappy. $25-45.
  Betsy Ross #709-6, 9 1/2" Bowl. $25-45.
  Betsy Ross #709-17, 6" h. Compote. $25-40.
  Hobnail #718-27, 11 1/2" Crimped Bowl. $25-45.
  #754-1, 7 1/2" h. Vase. $20-30.
  Hobnail #718-6, 9" 2-Handled Salad Bowl. $25-45.
  Williamsburg #708-61, 7" h. Handled Urn Vase. $20-30.
Bottom Row, Left to Right:
  Hobnail #718-10, 6 1/2" Nappy. $10-20.
  Betsy Ross #709-9, 7 oz. Cream. $30-45.
  Betsy Ross #709-10, 7 oz. Sugar and Cover. $30-45.
  #730-1, 7" Duck Ash Tray. $20-35.
  Homestead #63-3, 4 1/2" Nappy. $10-15.
  Betsy Ross #709-15, 4" Nappy. $10-15.
  Hobnail #718-21, 3 1/2" h. Jam Jar and Cover. $20-35.
  #786-1, 6" h. Vase. $15-25.
  Grape #719-1, 7 1/2" Nappy. $20-30.
  Hobnail #718-10, 6 1/2" Nappy. $10-20.
  Hobnail #718-11, 6" 2-Part Relish. $10-20.

Bottom: Top Row, Left to Right:
  Betsy Ross #709-14, 7" h. Candlestick. $30-45.
  Betsy Ross #709-4, 7 1/2" h. Urn Vase. $25-35.
  Hobnail #718-16, 5" Footed Ivy Bowl. $25-35.
  Hobnail #718-18, 4 " h. Footed Crimped Compote. $25-35.
  Grape #719-11, 6" h. Vase. $25-40.
  Betsy Ross #709-11, 9 1/2" Compote. $30-45.
  Grape #719-6, 52 oz. Jug. $45-65.
  Homestead #763-5, 6" h. Vase. $20-30.
Bottom Row, Left to Right:
  American Way #771-1, 6 1/2" h. Vase. $45-65.
  Hobnail #718-25, 4 1/2" Candlestick. $15-20.
  Williamsburg #708-31, 6" Handled Compote. $35-55.
  Homestead #763-2, 9" Bowl. $30-45.
  Hobnail #718-24, 5 oz. Sugar. $15-25.
  Hobnail #718-23, 5 oz. Cream. $15-25.
  Grape #719-10, Ivy Bowl. $15-25.
  Grape #719-7, 8 oz. Tumbler. $10-15.

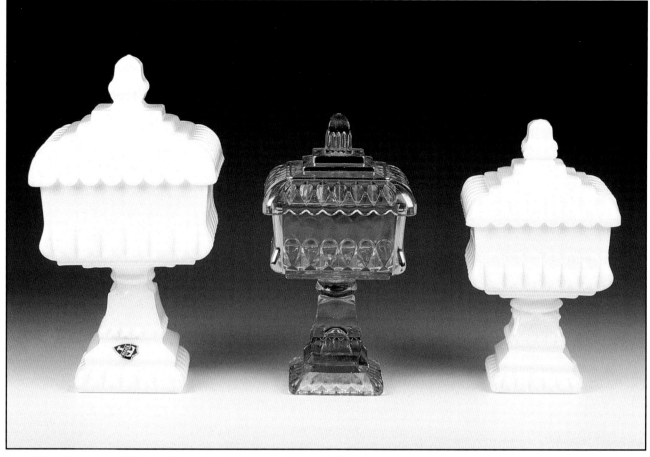

Tiffin, Milk Glass #712-2, 9 1/2" Wedding Bowl and Cover. $25-45.
Jeannette Glass, 8 1/4" Wedding Bowl and Cover.
Westmoreland Glass Company, 8 1/4" Wedding Bowl and Cover.

The Wedding Bowl originated as part of the Crystal Wedding pattern glass line produced by Adams and Co. of Pittsburgh, Pennsylvania. Crystal Wedding was designed and patented by James B. Lyon in 1875. Production of the Crystal Wedding pattern was continued by the United States Glass Company after Adams and Co. joined the corporation in 1891. Most Crystal Wedding is found in Crystal, Crystal with ruby stain, or with copper wheel engraving.

The United States Glass Company reissued the Wedding Bowl in three sizes, 12" h., 10" h., and 6 1/2" h., c. 1957. The 6 1/2" h. size was called a cigarette box. These were available in Milk Glass, Crystal, Crystal with blue or ruby stain, Gold Stipple, and Golden Nineties decoration. All these items were produced at Glassport.

In 1961, the 10" h. Wedding Bowl, and the 6 1/2" h. Cigarette Box were offered in Plum and Golden Banana. These two colors were produced at Factory R, Tiffin.

The Westmoreland, Jeannette, and L.E. Smith Glass Companies offered very similar pieces and listed them as wedding bowls or wedding jars. As early as 1956, Jeannette produced two sizes of wedding bowls, 8" h. and 6 1/2" h. in blue, crystal, crystal with gold, green, and shell pink. L.E. Smith offered a milk glass wedding jar in their 1961 catalog, measuring 8" h. and 4" square.

Westmoreland Glass offered three sizes of wedding bowls, 10" h., 8" h., and 6" h. Colors and decorations offered were: Crystal, Crystal with ruby stain, Milk Glass, and handpainted Milk Glass. An easy way to differentiate between the companies is to study the differences in the finials, as shown in the photos.

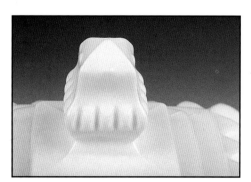

Detail of Tiffin finial. The Tiffin finial is more 'notched' at the bottom of the finial than the Westmoreland finial.

Detail of Jeannette Glass finial. The Jeannette finial has a series of vertical lines.

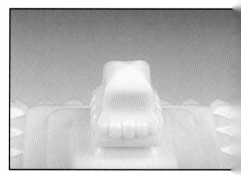

Detail of Westmoreland finial. The Westmoreland finial has a series of side-by-side ovals near the bottom edge.

Crystal with allover gold decoration #15179, 4 3/4" Handled Compote. Produced c. 1959. $25-45.

Golden Banana #8212, 6 1/2" Cigarette Box. $45-65.
Plum #8212, 6 1/2" Cigarette Box. $45-65.

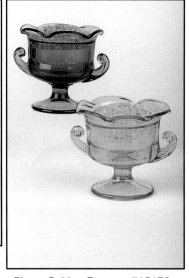

Plum, Golden Banana #15179, 4 3/4" Handled Compotes with Crystal Flower Blocks. $35-55 each.

#9441 5 1/2" Nite Lamp, also referred to as Old Fashion "Courtin' or Bundlin' Lamp."
  Plum. $90-115.
  Golden Banana. $90-115.
  Crystal with ruby stain. $90-115.
  Also produced in Milk Glass. $45-65.

Black 5" Aster Bowl. These were produced in the 1970s, and are identical in design to the #16273 Aster Bowls dating from the 1920s, however they are heavier in weight. This piece is signed with the acid-stamped Tiffin Shield on the bottom. $45-65.

"Pink" 6 1/2" h. Iris Vase, crimped top. $45-65.
Smoke 6 1/2" h. Iris Vase, rounded top. $35-55.
Smoke 6 1/2" h. Iris Vase, crimped top. $35-55.
   These items were produced in the 1970s, in bright or satin finish, and are signed with the acid-stamped Tiffin Shield on the base. These are thinner, and lighter in weight, than the 1920s #16254 iris vases. Also produced in Black. $45-65.

Black, Crystal, Amber #6324, 3 1/4" Cinderella Slippers.
   The Crystal Cinderella Slipper was first produced for the January 1954 Glass Trade Show in Pittsburgh. The Black slipper is sometimes found with a satin finish and also dates from the 1950s. A limited edition of 58 Cobalt slippers were produced in 1989 by the Dalzell-Viking Glass Company for the Tiffin Glass Collectors Club. These were acid-stamped TGCC on the bottom, so as not to confuse them with the originals.
      Black $110-135 pair.
      Crystal $90-115 pair.
      Amber $110-135 pair.
      Cobalt (repro) $50-75 pair.

1933 United States Glass Company catalog page.
#32362 Modernistic Dispenser. $300-350.

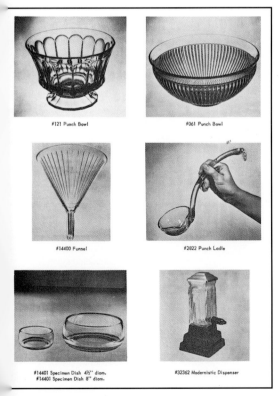

#121 Punch Bowl   #061 Punch Bowl

#14400 Funnel   #2822 Punch Ladle

#14401 Specimen Dish 4½'' diam.
#14401 Specimen Dish 8'' diam.   #32362 Modernistic Dispenser

1958 United States Glass Company catalog
page, reintroducing the #32362 Modernistic
Dispenser.

Milk Glass #725, 7 piece Berry Set. (8" and 4" Bowls). Produced 1960. $55-75
set.

Crystal #15310, Footed Flower Arranger. $20-35.
    These are nearly identical in form to the satin glass fan vases from the 1920s
and 1930s, but they appear to be a little more elongated. Produced in 1960
at Glassport.

Milk Glass #75310, Footed Flower Arranger. $35-55.
Produced in 1960 at Glassport.

Lincoln Continental Mark IV opera window. Tiffin Glass and Mirror of Tiffin, Ohio, cut the oval glass for the windows. The Tiffin Glass factory then cut the silver leaf Continental star on over 60,000 of these windows in 1971 for the Ford Motor Company.

1971 promotional photograph for the Lincoln Continental Mark IV opera window.

1968 Tiffin Glass catalog page.

The items shown on these 1968 catalog pages are items which were produced at a Clarksburg, West Virginia glass factory owned by the Continental Can Corporation. Continental Can purchased the Hazel Atlas factory, located in Clarksburg in 1964, prior to purchasing the Tiffin Art Glass Company in June 1966. These are pressed items, marketed as Tiffinware, to capitalize on the established Tiffin Glass name.

1968 Tiffin Glass catalog page.

1968 Tiffin Glass catalog page.

1968 Tiffin Glass catalog page.

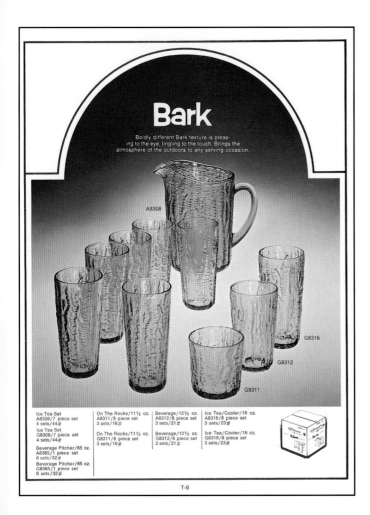

Bark

Boldly different Bark texture is pleasing to the eye, tingling to the touch. Brings the atmosphere of the outdoors to any serving occasion.

A8308

G8316

G8312

G8311

Ice Tea Set A8308/7 piece set 4 sets/44#	On The Rocks/11½ oz. A8311/8 piece set 3 sets/16#	Beverage/12½ oz. A8312/8 piece set 3 sets/21#	Ice Tea/Cooler/16 oz. A8316/8 piece set 3 sets/23#
Ice Tea Set G8308/7 piece set 4 sets/44#	On The Rocks/11½ oz. G8311/8 piece set 3 sets/16#	Beverage/12½ oz. G8312/8 piece set 3 sets/21#	Ice Tea/Cooler/16 oz. G8316/8 piece set 3 sets/23#
Beverage Pitcher/65 oz. A8365/1 piece set 6 sets/32#			
Beverage Pitcher/65 oz. G8365/1 piece set 6 sets/32#			

Bark

Boldly masculine Bark, interesting to the touch with its textured surface and substantial look, perfect for casual entertaining.

A8324

A8327

| Footed Ash Tray A8327/1 piece set 12 sets/28# (gift box) | Tankard Mug/13 oz. A8324/4 piece set 3 sets/21# (in 2 pc. gift box) |
| Footed Ash Tray G8327/1 piece set 12 sets/28# (gift box) | Tankard Mug/13 oz. G8324/4 piece set 3 sets/21# (in 2 pc. gift box) |

DECORATED
Tankard Mugs

Hearty and handsome tankard mugs of white opal glass with the surface interest and sophistication of applied dimensional decor.

Decorative, removable self-coaster base of imported cork.

BREWER'S GARDEN

CONTEMPO

SPANISH SCROLL

8141

8140

Decorated Tankard Mugs/13 oz.
8104/1802/4 piece set
3 sets/16#
(one decoration per 4 piece set, three assorted decorations per master carton)

Beverage with Removable Cork Base/11 oz.
8141/8 piece set
3 sets/23#

Rocks with Removable Cork Base/8 oz.
8140/8 piece set
3 sets/20#

EMPIRE
DECORATED TUMBLERS

A new dimension in rich, imaginatively decorated tumblers with the surface interest and the look of sculptured design.

8937/2057

8937/2036

8937/2050

8937/2041

8937/2081

8936/2081

8936/2041

8936/2050 Rocks 3 sets/24# 8937/2050 Beverage 3 sets/26# "FLORENTINE" Textured blue scroll pattern with rich gold in two dimension	8936/2041 Rocks 3 sets/24# 8937/2041 Beverage 3 sets/26# "ANDALUSIA" Beautiful delicate gold panels with textured green vertical accents
8936/2037 Rocks 3 sets/24# 8937/2037 Beverage 3 sets/26# "CATHEDRAL" Smartly styled patterns of transparent greens with textured black accent	8936/2081 Rocks 3 sets/24# 8937/2081 Beverage 3 sets/26# "PLATINUM BANDS" Striking classic simplicity harmonious with both formal and informal table settings
8936/2036 Rocks 3 sets/24# 8937/2036 Beverage 3 sets/26# "SWIRL" Contemporary mod shapes in yellow green and red transparent colors with complimentary outline of antique gold.	

1968 Tiffin Glass catalog page.

Chapter 10
Tiffin Selections

The Tiffin Selections were introduced in 1961 in the Plum, Golden Banana and Empire Green colors. In 1962, Empire Green was dropped from the listing, and Twilight, Cobalt Blue, and Tiffin Rose were added. In addition to new colors being added in 1962, several new shapes were also introduced. The Tiffin Selections items, which are blown, are included to illustrate that Tiffin Glass was producing both pressed and blown ware during the same time frame, and in the same colors. This line is very popular with collectors today.

Golden Banana #6125, 4 3/4" h. Candle, bubble stem, with 8 1/2" h. diamond optic hurricane shade. $75-100 set.

Golden Banana #6110, 7 3/4" h. Compote. $125-150.
Cobalt Blue with Crystal trim #6109, 7 1/4" h. Compote. $150-175.
Golden Banana #6111, 5 3/4" Compote. $90-115.
Plum #6107, 6 1/2" h. Compote. $110-135.
Plum #6109, 7 1/4" h. Compote. $125-150.
Twilight #6110, 7 3/4" h. Compote. $150-175.
   All items have diamond optic.

Plum #6207, 12 1/2" h. Bud Vase. $75-100.
Plum #6100, 12" h. Candle. $65-85.
Golden Banana #6100, 8" h. Candle. $55-75.
Plum #6114, 10 3/4" h. Bud Vase, festoon optic. $45-65.
Crystal #6100, 12" h. Candle. $25-45.
Golden Banana #6100, 10" h. Candle. $55-75.

Plum #6101, 7 1/2" h. Candle, with 5 1/2" h.
  Hurricane Shade. $100-125 set.
Golden Banana #6101, 7 1/2" Candle, with 5 1/
  2" h. Hurricane Shade. $100-125 set.
Plum #6102, 4" h. Candle, with 8 1/2" h.
  Hurricane Shade. $75-100 set.
    The #6102 style of candle was designed by
  Ed Wormley. All hurricane shades have
  diamond optic.

Twilight #6101, 7 1/2" h. Candle. $85-110.
Plum #6101, 7 1/2" h. Candle. $45-65.
Cobalt Blue with Crystal trim #6101, 7 1/2" h.
  Candle. $85-110.
Golden Banana #6101, 7 1/2" h. Candle. $45-65.
Tiffin Rose #6101, 7 1/2" h. Candle. $85-110.

Tiffin Rose #6121, 10 3/4" h. Large Ivy Bowl.
  $100-125.
Plum #6120, 10" h. Small Ivy Bowl. $75-100.
Golden Banana #6121, 10 3/4" h. Large Ivy
  Bowl. $75-100.
Cobalt Blue with Crystal trim #6120, 10" h. Small
  Ivy Bowl. $165-190.
Golden Banana #6120, 10" h. Small Ivy Bowl.
$75-100.
Plum #6121, 10 3/4" h. Large Ivy Bowl. $75-100.
  All ivy bowls have diamond optic.

Plum #6103, 9 1/2" h. Candy Box and Cover. $125-150.
Golden Banana #6103, 9 1/2" h. Candy Box and Cover. $125-150.
Tiffin Rose # 6103, 9 1/2" h. Candy Box and Cover. $150-175.
    All candy boxes have diamond optic.

Cobalt Blue with Crystal trim #6116, 9 3/4" h. Bud Vase. $100-125.
Tiffin Rose with satin finish #6116, 9 3/4" h. Bud Vase. $65-85.
Tiffin Rose #6116, 9 3/4" h. Bud Vase. $65-85.
Golden Banana #6116, 9 3/4" h. Bud Vase. $45-65.
    All bud vases have festoon optic. Also produced in Twilight, Plum and Empire Green.

Cobalt Blue with Crystal trim #6106, 11 1/2" h. Candy Box and Cover. $200-225.
Golden Banana #6106, 11 1/2" h. Candy Box and Cover. $150-175.
    Both items have diamond optic. Also available in Plum and Empire Green.

Tiffin Rose #6123, 6" h. Small Rose Bowl. $85-110.
Tiffin Rose #6122, 7 1/2" h. Large Rose Bowl. $85-110.
Twilight #6123, 6" h. Small Rose Bowl. $125-150.
Golden Banana #6123, 6" h. Small Rose Bowl. $55-75.
Plum #6123, 6" h. Small Rose Bowl. $55-75.
    All rose bowls have diamond optic.

Plum:
#6127, 9 1/2" Center Bowl. $125-150.
#6128, 11 3/4" h. Vase. $150-175.
#6135, 7 1/2" h. Sweet Pea Vase. $150-175.
#6129, 11" h. Teardrop Vase. $150-175.
   All items have a bubble stem and diamond optic.

Golden Banana #6113, 10 3/4" h.
   Candy Jar and Cover, diamond optic.
   $125-150.
Golden Banana #6112, 8" h. Bud Vase.
   $35-55.
Plum #6112, 10" h. Bud Vase. $45-65.
Golden Banana #6112, 12" h. Bud
   Vase. $45-65.

Golden Banana #6133, 12" h. Vase. $150-175.
Cobalt Blue with Crystal trim #6132, 8" Rose Bowl. $225-250.
Cobalt Blue with Crystal trim #6133, 12" h. Vase. $225-250.
   All items have a bubble stem and diamond optic.

Tiffin Rose #6202, 12 1/2" h. Vase.
   $175-200.
Golden Banana #6135, 7 1/2" h. Sweet
   Pea Vase, bubble stem. $150-175.
Cobalt Blue with Crystal trim #6210, 12
   3/4" h. Vase, with gold paint decora-
   tion. $225-250.
   All items have diamond optic.

Golden Banana #6205, 10 1/2" h. Vase, diamond optic. $150-175.

Golden Banana #6132, 8" Rose Bowl, bubble stem, diamond optic. $150-175.

Golden Banana #6134, 10 1/2" h. Tub Vase, bubble stem, diamond optic. $150-175.

Golden Banana #6202, 12 1/2" h. Vase, diamond optic. $150-175.

Tiffin Rose #6200, 11 3/8" h. Bridal Cup, diamond optic. $125-150.
Plum #6200, 11 3/8" h. Bridal Cup, diamond optic. $100-125.
Also produced in Golden Banana, and Cobalt Blue with Crystal trim.

Tiffin Rose #6203, 9" h. Rose Bowl. $175-200.
Tiffin Rose #6210, 12 3/4" h. Vase. $175-200.
Cobalt Blue with Crystal trim #6203, 9" h. Rose Bowl. $225-250.
All have diamond optic.

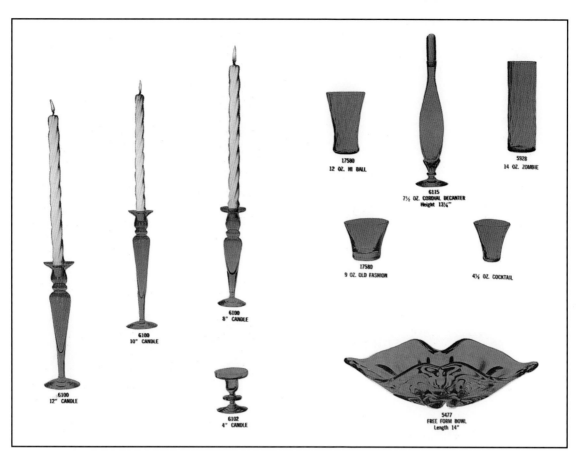

1961 Tiffin Selections pamphlet. The colors shown are Plum, Golden Banana, and Empire Green.

1961 Tiffin Selections pamphlet.

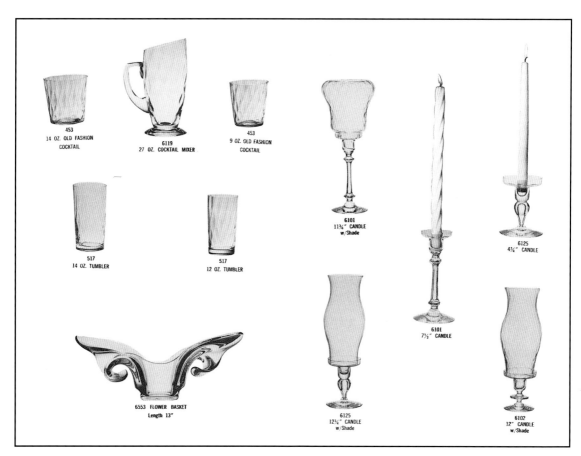

1961 Tiffin Selections pamphlet.

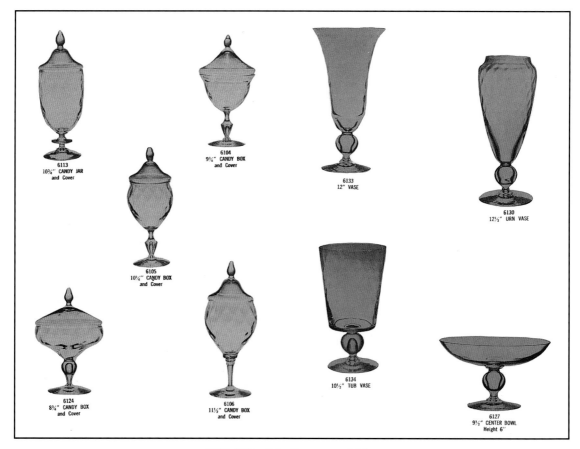

1961 Tiffin Selections pamphlet.

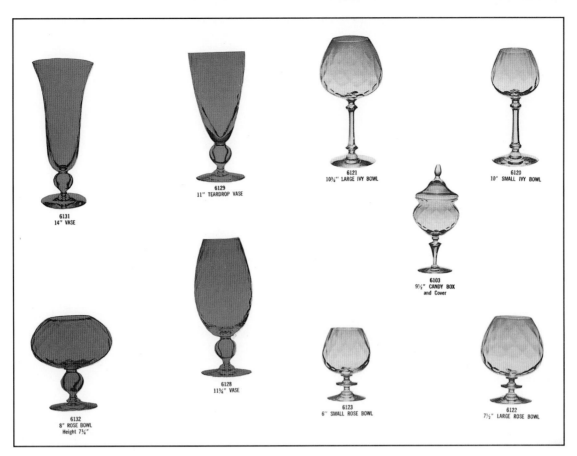

1961 Tiffin Selections pamphlet.

#6204, 11 3/4" h. Vase.
Introduced in January
1962, in Plum, Golden
Banana, Tiffin Rose, and
Cobalt Blue with Crystal
trim.

1961 Tiffin Selections pamphlet.

Chapter 11
Figurals

Both pressed and blown figurals were included in Tiffin's production, dating from 1945-1980. Joe Kreutz, Johnnie Fleming, and Paul Hoover are credited with making many of the early hand-fashioned pheasants, fish, and geese. Two of the very desirable pressed figurals are the "Chinese Monk" and the Persian Bookends. The popular Pall Mall swans were produced from Duncan and Miller molds.

Crystal #6042-1, 12 1/2" Pheasant, tail down.
Crystal #6042-2, 13" Pheasant, tail up. $200-250 pair.

Copen Blue #6042-2, 16" Pheasant, tail up.
Copen Blue #6042-1, 16" Pheasant, tail down. $500-550 pair.

Crystal #6042-1, 13" Pheasant, tail down.
Crystal #6042-2, 13" Pheasant, tail up.
    Both with controlled bubbles. $400-450 pair.

Twilight #6042-1, 17" Pheasant, tail down.
Twilight #6042-2, 18" Pheasant, tail up.
    The male pheasant with the tail raised, and the female with the tail lowered, have different line numbers. $1500-1750 pair.

Crystal 12 3/4" Pheasant. The tail on this pheasant has been split into three sections, something a glass worker would have done on his own time, not a production item. $200-250.

Assortment of production and nonproduction pheasants.

Small Pheasant Whimseys:
Wistaria and Crystal, 7 1/2". $250-300.
Crystal, 8". $150-175.
Smoke and Crystal, 7 1/2". $200-250.

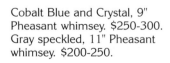

Cobalt Blue and Crystal, 9" Pheasant whimsey. $250-300. Gray speckled, 11" Pheasant whimsey. $200-250.

Crystal 10" Rooster. Not a production item. This was fashioned from a pheasant figurine. $200-250.

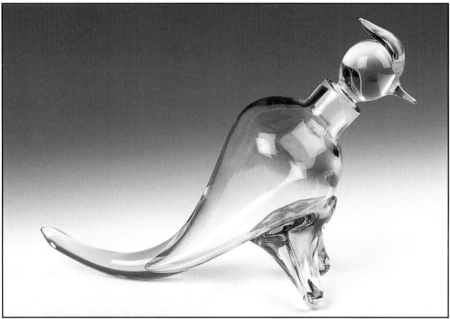

Wild Rose #5507, 11" Pheasant Decanter with Crystal stopper. This item was listed as an Oil/Vinegar or Cordial Decanter, 1955. The body is made from the #5507 Cornucopia mold. $200-250.

Crystal #6043, 9" Fish, c. 1946. $400-450. Also produced in Copen Blue. $700-750.

Crystal 13" Fish, c. 1946. This figurine has some of the same elements as the #6043 fish. The base, eyes, mouth, tail, and fins look the same. The body was simply elongated. The elongated fish was not a production item. $550-600.

Crystal #6044, 9" Goose, c. 1946. The left Goose is the most commonly found pose. In addition to the bent-neck pose, there is a Goose with its head close to the ground. The thickness and weight of the Goose figurine will vary widely. $400-450.

Copen Blue #6044, 9" Goose. $700-750. Wistaria 5 1/2" h. paperweight Goose whimsey. $300-350.

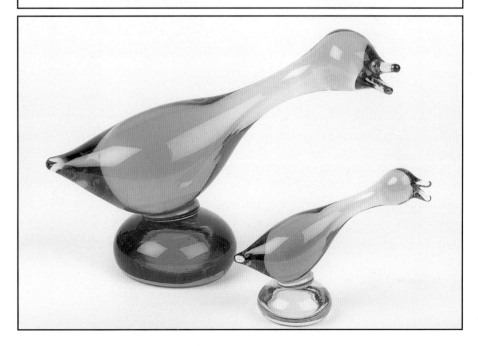

Opal and Crystal 10 1/4" h. "Chinese Monk" figurines, undocumented line number. These date to c. 1949 and were also reportedly produced in Black, with a production of 1000 in each color. These are extremely difficult to find. Opal. $900-1000. Crystal. $750-850.

Killarney #6320, 7 1/2" h. Burmese Bookends.

These bookends appear black in color because of the thickness of the glass. Under a very strong light, the face will glow red, while the rest of the piece will shine a dark green. This item appeared in a 1952 price listing, wholesaling for $36.00 per dozen. $500-600 pair.

Crystal with satin finish #6320, 7 1/2" h. Burmese Bookend. $200-250 pair.
Also produced in Crystal with bright finish. $150-200 pair.

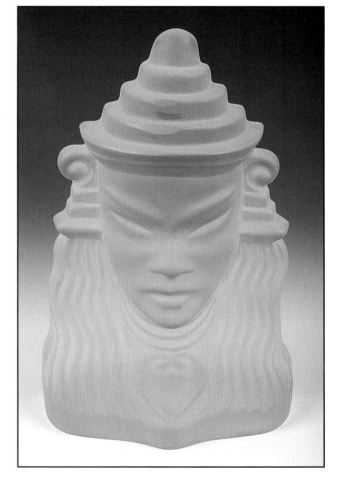

Crystal #5905-20, 14 1/2" Floater
with Fawn and Vase.
   The fawn and the vase have the
same detail at the base. The vase
insert is extremely rare. The Floater
with Fawn was designed by the
firm of Pipsan-Saarinen-Swanson.
$90-115 set.

Copen Blue 14 1/2" Floater with 10" h.
Fawn, c. 1965.
   When sold singly, the floater line
number is #5905, and the fawn line
number is #6322. $275-325 set.

Copen Blue and Crystal with satin
finish #5905-20, 14 1/2" Floater
with Fawn. $150-175 set.

Smoke #6322, 10" Fawn. This color
was probably not a production
item. $65-85.

Citron Green #5905-20, 14 1/2"
Floater with Fawn. c. 1965.
   In 1999, there were 100 Floaters
with Fawns produced in a vaseline
color for a private individual by the
Summit Art Glass Company in
Ravenna, Ohio, who currently
owns the mold. The vaseline color
is similar in appearance to Citron.
$250-300 set.

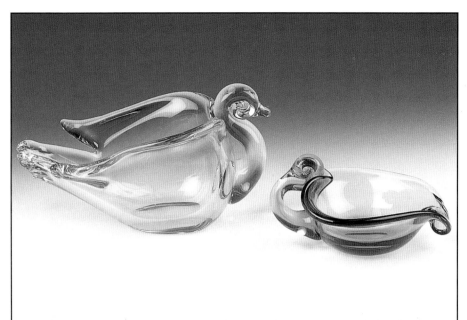

Twilight #5401, 10" Drake Bowl, c. 1954. $400-450.

Wistaria #5400, 6" Bon Bon with Sleeping Duck handle, c. 1954. $150-175.

Pall Mall. Ruby:

#30-83, 12" Swan. $100-125.
#30-82, 10 1/2" Swan. $55-75.
#30-81, 7" Swan. $35-55.
#30-80, 3 1/2" Swan. $65-85.
The measurements given are catalog measurements. The actual measurements will vary up to an inch more.

Stacked set of Ruby Pall Mall Swans.

Assortment of sizes and colors of Pall Mall Swans. The Pall Mall Swan was originally a Duncan and Miller Glass Company mold. The Ruby, Crystal, and Green colors were also produced by Duncan and Miller, in five sizes: 3 1/2", 6", 7", 10 1/2" and 12".

#30-82, 12" Swan (Ruby, Green, Crystal, Copen Blue, Desert Red, Smoke, Citron Green, Greenbriar) $100-125. $75-95. $15-25. $75-95. $30-50. $30-40. $30-50. $30-40.

#30-82, 10 1/2" Swan (Ruby, Green, Crystal, Copen Blue, Desert Red, Smoke, Citron Green, Greenbriar) $55-75. $45-65. $15-25. $45-65. $30-50. $25-35. $30-50. $25-35.

#30-81, 7" Swan (Ruby, Green, Crystal, Copen Blue, Desert Red, Smoke, Citron Green, Greenbriar) $35-55. $30-50. $10-20. $30-50. $25-45. $20-30. $25-45. $20-30.

#30-80, 3 1/2" Swan (Ruby, Green, Crystal, Copen Blue, Desert Red, Smoke, Citron Green, Greenbriar) $65-85. $55-75. $15-25. $55-75. $45-65. $35-55. $45-65. $35-55.

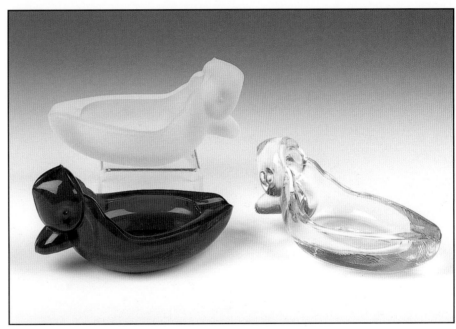

Pall Mall.
Cobalt Blue #30-101, 4" Duck Ash Tray. $45-65.
"Pink" with satin finish #30-101, 4" Duck Ash Tray. $25-35.
"Pink" #30-101, 4" Duck Ash Tray. $25-35.
Also produced in Desert Red, $25-35. Black. $25-35.
Produced from a Duncan and Miller Glass Company mold.

Plum #562-1, 12 1/2" Swan Flower Arranger.
$175-200.
Tiffin Rose #562-1, 12 1/2" Swan Flower Arranger. $225-250.
Golden Banana #562-1, 12 1/2" Swan Flower Arranger. $175-200.
    Also produced in Twilight. $300-350.
Produced from a Duncan and Miller Glass Company mold.

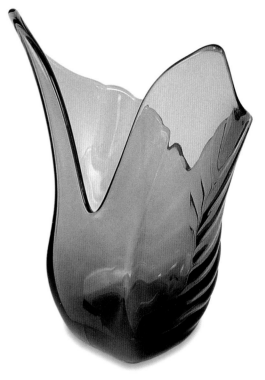

Plum #562-3, 9" Vase.
    This is the same shape as the 562-2 Swan Vase, minus the neck and head. $45-65.

Crystal #562-1, 12 1/2" Swan Flower Arranger. $75-100.
Tiffin Rose #562-2, 10 1/2" h. Swan Vase. $225-250.

Plum #562-1, 12 1/2" Swan Flower Arranger.
$175-200.
Plum #562-2, 10 1/2" h. Swan Vase. $175-200.

Top left: 1979 Tiffin Glass pamphlet featuring the Tiffin Duck and Madeira lines.

Top right: "Pink" #530-2, 9" Duck Candy Box and Cover. $45-65.
Beige Opal #530-2, 9" Duck Candy Box and Cover. $50-70.

The Westmoreland Glass Company and the Summit Art Glass Company have reproduced the duck candy box.

Center: Green Opal #530-2, 9" Duck Candy Box and Cover. $50-70.

The following information was included on a card which was packaged with the Tiffin Duck.

"In the archives of the Tiffin Glass Factory at Tiffin, Ohio, the 106 year old moulds were found which produced 'The Tiffin Duck'. This duck was originally produced at the Challinor, Taylor and Company factory in Tarentum, Pennsylvania. The Challinor facility began producing glass items in 1870 and remained in business as Challinor, Taylor and Co., until July 1, 1891 when it became part of the United States Glass Company, a combine of eighteen then-existing glass factories throughout Ohio, Pennsylvania and West Virginia. The duck mould was sent to the Glassport, Pennsylvania plant shortly after 1894. Glassport was then part of the United States Glass Company combine.

"In 1932, the then 62 year old mould was sent to the Tiffin Glass Plant, the most prestigious of all the United States Glass Companies. Upon close examination, 'The Duck' mould was found to be damaged. Tiffin's ingenious chief mouldmaker, however, was able to replace the damaged section with a metal plug which still remains in the mould. If you look closely at the underneath section of the tail on today's duck, you will see a neatly repaired rectangular patch. If you own one of the original ducks without such a patch mark, you can be sure that it was made prior to 1932 and is truly a bit of early Americana.

"Although the duck mould equipment is 106 years old, the detail today is still so realistic that you can almost see the feathers rippling as the duck settles over its nest. The intricate detail of the mould creates a fine example of American pressed glass for today's collector and of the workmanship done by the skilled craftsmen of the Tiffin Glass Factory…the oldest existing glass factory in America…built and in operation on its present site since 1887."

Bottom: Plum #530-2, 9" Duck Candy Box and Cover. $50-70.

Chapter 12
Paperweights and Whimseys

Some of the most beautiful items created by skilled Tiffin workers were the paperweights. The paperweights were fashioned by the workers after hours, as gifts for family and friends. Some were sold in the Outlet Store. The artists included: Victor LeMaire, Lucian Delvenne, Jake Querion, D. Edwards, Vincent "Mousie" Meier, Paul Sullivan, Orie Mitchell, Paul "Scratchy" Robbins, Tom Faris, William Wolf, and R. Conn. Among the items made were fruit weights, teapots, and a variety of animals. Many of the paperweights are marked with an acid-stamp, Tiffin Shield, or signed and dated by the artist. These non-production items were not widely distributed across the United States and therefore are difficult to find outside of the Tiffin, Ohio, area.

Most of the colors used for the paperweights were production colors; however, some small color batches were made in colors that did not have an official name. Generic color names, i.e. green, blue, pink, aqua are designated within quotation marks.

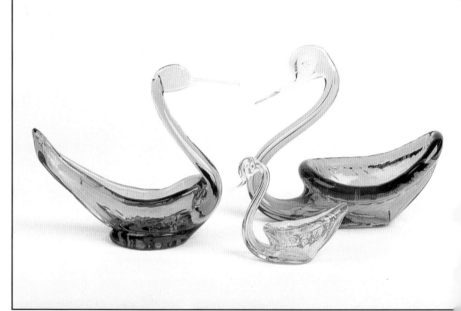

Top: **Ducks.**
　　Cobalt Blue 4 3/4". $40-55.
　　"Pink" 5". $35-50.
　　Milk Glass 3 1/2". $25-40.
　　Crystal 4". $20-35.
　　"Aqua" 4 1/2". $35-50.
　　Cornsilk 5". $35-50.
　　Smoke 5 1/4". $30-45.

Center: **Swans.**
　　Greenbriar 7".　$25-35.
　　Cornsilk 4". $20-30.
　　Desert Red 7 1/2". $25-35.

Bottom: **Swans.**
　　Plum 8 1/2". $100-125.
　　Plum 4". $75-95.
　　Black with Crystal wings 8 1/2" $100-125.
　　Cornsilk 8" $100-125.

Swans.
    Crystal 4". $35-55.
    "Pink" 5 1/2". $65-85.
    Ruby 6". $135-160.
    Ruby 8". $135-160.

Swans.
    Cornsilk 8". $100-125.
    Cobalt Blue 6". $125-150.
    "Aqua" 6 3/4" $100-125.

Black with Crystal wings, 8 1/2"
  Candleholder Swan. $100-125.

Twilight 4" Sparrow with controlled Bubbles. $150-175.

Desert Red and Crystal 4" Sparrow dated and signed, "1975, Orie Mitchell." $125-150.

Black and Crystal 5" Sparrow with Controlled Bubbles. $150-175.

Sparrows.
Cobalt Blue and Crystal, 3 1/4", controlled bubbles. $100-125. "Pink," 4" controlled bubbles. $75-100.

Twilight 5 1/4" Squirrel, 3 1/4" Mouse, attributed to Orie Mitchell, c. 1974. $125-150 each.

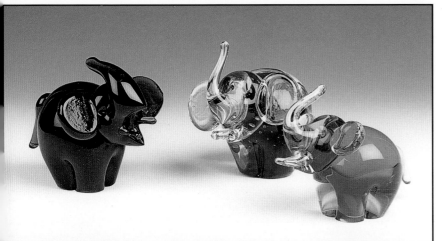

Elephants.
   Smoke 5". $125-150.
   Cobalt Blue and Crystal, 6 1/2", controlled
   bubbles. $150-200.
   "Pink" 4 1/2". $125-150.
      All of these made by Orie Mitchell.

Twilight 5 1/4" Squirrel. $125-150.
Blue 3 1/4" Sparrow, with controlled bubbles. $65-85.
Cobalt Blue 6 1/4" Porpoise. $100-125.
Pink 6 1/2" Porpoise. $85-110.

Whales.
   6" Green. $65-85.
   5 3/4" Cobalt Blue. $85-110.
   5" Pink. $65-85.
   5 1/2" Smoke. $65-85.
      Attributed to Orie Mitchell, some of the whales
      are artist signed.

This is another style of whale paperweight. The tail
is pointed back over the body. All of these are
signed with the acid-stamped Tiffin shield on the
bottom, and all have controlled bubbles.
   4 3/4" Desert Red and Crystal. $100-125.
   4 3/4" Cobalt Blue and Crystal. $125-150.
   4 3/4" Smoke and Crystal. $100-125.

Fish Whimseys.
   Blue 7". $75-100.
   Copen Blue 6 3/4". $75-100.
   Crystal 6 1/2". $65-85.
   Smoke 6 1/4". $75-100.

"Green" and Cobalt Blue, 4 3/4" Whale, controlled bubbles. $125-150.

Detail of acid-stamped Tiffin shield.

Standing Cat.
   Cobalt Blue 6" h. $65-85.
   Twilight 5" h. $85-110.
   Smoke 5" h. $35-55.
   Desert Red 4 3/4" h. $45-65.
   "Blue" 6" h. $45-65.
   Ruby 6 3/4" h. $65-85.
   The Viking Glass Company produced a cat exactly like the
Tiffin cats shown here. The head, body, and base are the same.
It may be possible that a glass worker labored at each glass
company at different times and that worker produced the same
style of cats for each company. The Standing Cats are attrib-
uted to Orie Mitchell.

Orie Mitchell.

Black and Crystal, 4 1/4" h. Penguin, controlled bubbles. $125-150.

"Blue" 6" h. Standing Cat. $45-65.
Twilight 5" h. Standing Cat. $85-110.
Crystal 4 1/2" Mouse. $55-75.
"Pink" 4" h. Cat Face. $45-65.

Black and Crystal 5 1/2" h. Bear. $100-125.
Copen Blue 5" h. Penguin. $150-175.

Detail of impressed Tiffin Shield on cog base.

Crystal 5 1/2" h. Owl. $65-85.
Crystal 5 1/2" h. Bear. $65-85.
Black and Crystal 4 1/4" Rabbit, controlled
 bubbles. $100-125.
    The owl has an impressed Tiffin shield on the
    underside. All three animals are attributed to
    Orie Mitchell.

Crystal 4" h. Pig. $65-85.
Crystal 4 1/4" Hippopotamus. $65-85.
Crystal 3 1/4" Rabbit. $45-65.
Crystal and Desert Red 3 3/4" h. Cat, controlled
 bubbles. $55-75.
    All are attributed to Orie Mitchell.

Smoke 4". $75-100.
"Green" and Crystal with
controlled bubbles 5".
$125-150.
Ruby 3 1/2". $100-125.
All with applied
bird.

Assortment of Fruit paperweights in various colors and shapes. A pear, apple, pumpkin, and strawberry comprise the four fruit weights.

Desert Red 4 1/2" h. Pumpkin. $65-85.
Desert Red 3" h. Strawberry. $55-75.
"Pink" 3 3/4" h. Strawberry. $55-75.
Crystal with applied green leaf 4 1/2" h. Pear. $55-75.
Milk Glass 2 3/4" h. Strawberry. $35-55.
Milk Glass 4 1/4" h. Pear. $45-65.
Crystal and Ruby 2 3/4" h. Strawberry. $55-75.
Cornsilk 4" h. Apple. $65-85.

Green 6" h. Pear. $65-85.
Green 4 1/2" h. Apple.
 $65-85.
Green 4 1/2" h. Small Pear.
 $55-75.
Cobalt Blue 4 1/2" h.
 Pumpkin. $85-110.
Cobalt Blue 4" h. Apple.
 $85-110.
    All with controlled
 bubbles.

Cobalt Blue and Crystal, with controlled bubbles:
   5" h. Pumpkin. $85-110.
   5 1/4" h. Pear. $85-110.
   5" h. Apple. $85-110.
   3 1/4" h. Strawberry. $75-100.

Twilight with controlled bubbles:
4" h. Apple. $85-110.
2 1/2" h. Strawberry. $75-100.
3 1/2" h. Pumpkin. $85-110.
4 1/2" h. Pear. $85-110.

Desert Red and Crystal 6 1/2" h. Pineapple, controlled bubbles. $85-110.
Twilight 6 1/4" h. Apple, applied leaf, controlled bubbles. $150-175.

Smoke and Crystal, 3 1/2", dated "1974." $55-75.
Killarney and Crystal, 31/2", with candleholder socket, signed "V. Meier, 1960." $75-100.
Desert Red and Crystal, 5 1/4" h., faceted, signed "O. Mitchell, and T. Faris, 1973." $200-225.
   All with controlled bubbles.

"Pink," 3" h., faceted, signed "V. Meier and W. Wolf 1973." $200-225.
Ruby and Crystal, 3" faceted, signed "W. Wolf and O. Mitchell, 1972." $225-250.
Ruby and Crystal, 2 3/4", faceted, signed "V. Meier and W. Wolf, 1972." $225-250.
   All with controlled bubbles.

Vincent "Mousie" Meier on ladder, and Dick Cook in the mold room at the Tiffin Glass factory.

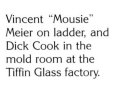

Black, 4 1/4" h., faceted, signed "W. Wolf and O. Mitchell, 1973." $175-200.

Twilight, 4" h., faceted, controlled bubbles, signed "W. Wolf and O. Mitchell, 1974." $225-250.

Green and Crystal, 5" h., signed "T. Faris and O. Mitchell, 1976." $175-200.

Greenbriar and Crystal, 4 1/4" h. $175-200.

Greenbriar and Cobalt Blue, 4 3/4" h., signed "T. Faris and O. Mitchell, 1975." $200-225.

    All with faceting and controlled bubbles.

Smoke and Crystal, 3 1/2" h., faceted, signed "W. Wolf and O. Mitchell, 1976." $200-225.

Blue and Crystal, 4 1/2". $175-200.

Smoke and Crystal, 5" h. faceted, signed "W. Wolf and O. Mitchell, 1976." $200-225.

    All with controlled bubbles.

Assortment of Tiffin Glass paperweights with faceting and controlled bubbles.

Black and Crystal, 5 3/4" h., signed "W. Wolf and O. Mitchell, 1973." $200-225.
Cobalt Blue and Crystal, 3 1/2" h. signed "W. Wolf and V. Meier, 1972." $200-225.
    Both with faceting and controlled bubbles.

"Aqua," 5" h., signed "T. Faris and O. Mitchell, 1974." $200-225.
"Aqua," 3 1/2" h., signed "T. Faris and O. Mitchell, 1974." $200-225.
    Both with faceting and controlled bubbles.

Smoke and Crystal, 3" h., signed "V. Meier and W. Wolf, 1970." $200-225.
Smoke and Crystal, 3" h., signed "V. Meier and W. Wolf, 1970." $200-225.
    Both with faceting and controlled bubbles.

"Green," 5" h., signed "T. Faris and O. Mitchell, 1976." $175-200.
"Green," 3" h., signed "W. Wolf and O. Mitchell, 1978." $175-200.
  Both with controlled bubbles and faceting.

Ruby and Crystal, 3 3/4" h., signed "V. Meier and W. Wolf, 1970." $225-250.
Ruby and Crystal, 3 1/2" h., signed "V. Meier and W. Wolf, 1970." $225-250.
  Both with faceting and controlled bubbles.

"Pink" 3 3/4" h., signed "V. Meier and W. Wolf, 1973." $200-225.
"Pink" 3" h., signed "O. Mitchell and R. Conn, 1974." $200-225.
  Both with faceting and controlled bubbles.

Plum and Crystal, 3 3/8" faceted. $200-225.
Plum and Crystal, 2 3/8" faceted. $200-225.
Plum and Crystal, 3 1/2". $175-200.

Faceted "Window" Weights.
Ruby and Crystal, 2 3/4", signed "W. Wolf and O. Mitchell, 1975." $225-250.
Black and Crystal, 3 1/4" h., controlled bubbles. $200-225.
Smoke and Desert Red, 3 1/4", controlled bubbles, signed "O. Mitchell and T. Faris, 1975." $200-225.

Black and Crystal, 4" h., faceted, signed "V. Meier and W. Wolf, 1970." $175-200.
Smoke and Crystal, 3 1/2", dated 1974. $175-200
Black and Crystal, 5 3/4" h., faceted, signed "W. Wolf and O. Mitchell, 1973." $175-200.
Smoke and Crystal, 5" h., faceted, signed "W. Wolf and O. Mitchell, 1976." $175-200.
Smoke and Crystal, 3" h., faceted, signed "W. Wolf and O. Mitchell, 1970." $175-200.
All with controlled bubbles.

Ruby and Crystal, 3", signed W. Wolf and O.
   Mitchell, 1972. $225-250.
Ruby and Crystal, 3 3/4", signed W. Wolf and V.
   Meier, 1970. $225-250.
Ruby and Crystal, 2 1/2". $225-250.
      All with faceting and controlled bubbles.

"Pink," 3 3/4" h., signed "V. Meier and W. Wolf,
   1973." $200-225.
"Aqua," 5" h., signed "O. Mitchell and T. Faris,
   1974." $200-225.
Cornsilk, 3" h., signed "O. Mitchell and T. Faris,
   1972." $200-225.
      All with faceting and controlled bubbles.

"Copper Blue" and Crystal, 3 1/4" h., controlled
   bubbles. $150-175.
Wistaria, 3" h., faceted. $200-225.
"Green" and Crystal, 5" h., faceted, controlled
   bubbles, signed "T. Faris and O. Mitchell, 1976."
   $200-225.
Killarney and Crystal, 3 1/2", with candleholder
   socket, signed "V. Meier, 1960." $75-100.
"Pink" 3", controlled bubbles, cog base. $75-100.

Copen Blue, 4 1/2" h. $75-100.
Black and Crystal, 5" h. $75-100.
Wistaria, 3 1/2" h. $125-150.
    All with controlled bubbles.

"Copper Blue" and Crystal, 3 1/4" h. $150-175.
"Copper Blue," 3" h. $150-175.
    Both with controlled bubbles, and signed "Paul Robbins, 1971."

Smoke and Crystal, 5 5/8" h. Candleholder, controlled bubbles.
    $100-125.
Twilight, 3 1/4", with mica flecks. $175-200.

Cornsilk and Cobalt Blue, 9" Bud Vase whimsey, with controlled bubbles. Signed "O. Mitchell, 1974." $75-100.

Millefiori.
  2 3/4" 'Girlie
    1948'.
  2 3/4" 'To Bud
    from Jake'.
  2 3/4" 'Chas.
    Detrick 1948'.
  Attributed to Jake
    Querion.

Millefiori.
  2 3/4" Ash Tray. $75-100.
  2 1/2" h. Inkwell Paperweight. $75-100.
  The ash tray is attributed to Jake Querion.

143

Teapots.
"Copper Blue," 6",
  signed "O.
  Mitchell."
  $75-100.
"Pink," 5 1/2".
  $75-100.
Cobalt Blue and
  Crystal, 6".
  $100-125.
Cobalt Blue and
  Crystal, 5 1/2".
  $100-125.
All with controlled
  bubbles, and
  acid-stamped
  Tiffin shield on
  base.

Teapots.
  "Pink," 5 1/2" with controlled bubbles. $75-100.
  "Aqua," 5", with controlled bubbles. $75-100.
  Black and Crystal, 5 1/2", with controlled bubbles. $75-100.
  Cobalt Blue, 5 1/2". $100-125.

Teapot. Citron Green, 6 1/4", with Air Trap design. $75-100.

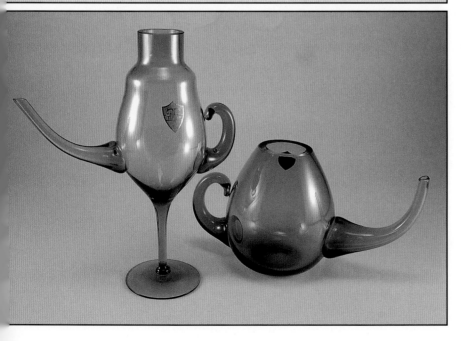

Teapots.
   Desert Red, 5". $75-100.
   Blue and Crystal, 5", signed "O. Mitchell, '74." $75-100.
   Greenbriar, 5", signed "O. Mitchell, '74." $65-85.
      All with controlled bubbles.

"Green," 8" h. footed Teapot whimsey; 8" d. Teapot whimsey. $45-65 each.
   Also produced in Black. $45-65 each.

Cone 8" h. Paperweight with Ruby spiral. $225-250.
Small 3" h. Tree Paperweight with pink colored branches. $125-150.
Large 6 1/2" h. Tree Paperweight with multicolored branches. $200-225.

Detail of Cone Paperweight.

Detail of small Tree Paperweight.

Detail of large Tree paperweight.

Crystal:
  3 1/4" h. engraved Prism. $200-225.
  6 3/4" h. engraved Prism, flower urn. $300-350.
  3 1/4" h. engraved Prism. $200-225.
  All attributed to Lucian Delvenne.

Detail of large prism with flower urn.

Detail of engraving on the small left hand prism.

Detail of engraving on the small right hand prism.

Detail of Chalice engraving.

"Orange/Pink," 7 3/4" h. Prism paperweight with engraved chalice. Prism sits on a square base. $300-350.

Top right: Detail of Twilight Prism paperweight, showing urn with bouquet of flowers.

Twilight, 4 1/4" h. Prism paperweight. Engraved by Lucian Delvenne. $400-450.

Crystal with cranberry stain, 7" Cologne. The cordial goblet is encased in the Crystal hexagonal body with engraved edges. The 6-sided cut stopper has a controlled bubble. A very limited number of these were made and were attributed to Victor Hendrix and Victor LeMaire, c. 1940s. Reportedly, a few of these were made with a blue or green stained cordial goblet encased in Crystal. $900-1100.

Cologne with stopper removed.

Crystal, 6" h. Waterdrops, one with controlled bubbles. These were a special order for a Dayton, Ohio, water company. $45-65 each.

Smoke and Crystal, 24" swords, attributed to Orie Mitchell, c. 1970s. $175-200 each.

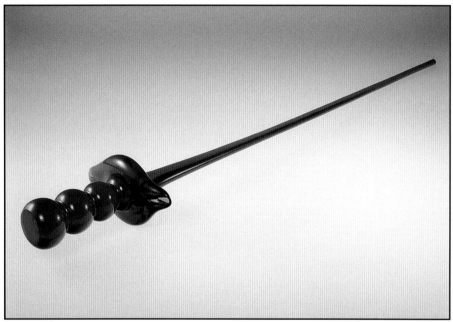

Cobalt Blue, 26 1/2" Sword, attributed to Orie Mitchell, c. 1974. The swords are very hard to find, and can be found in other colors as well. $225-250.

Crystal, 12" Hammer. $35-55.
Ruby and Crystal, 7 3/4" Hammer. $45-65.
Crystal, 9" Hammer. $35-55.
    Attributed to Orie Mitchell.

Center: Ruby and Crystal, 39" spiral-twist cane. $250-300.

Bottom: **Reproduction Cane.**
   The cane pictured here is one of several styles and colors that started to show up on the secondary market in late 1999. Other colors seen are ruby, cobalt, and dark green, usually having a contrasting colored stripe on them. A walking stick is also often seen in the colors listed above. Both the canes and walking sticks sport an oversized Tiffin label, about 1 1/2" in length. The fake Tiffin label is believed to be computer generated, with a patina added to it, to make it look old. It is unknown who is making the canes or the fake labels. The canes were heavily concentrated in Ohio to begin with, but there are now reports of them nationwide. Another telling point is that the canes are all in excellent condition. It is rather unusual to find an old cane in tip-top shape, as they were often carried by workers who marched in Labor Day Parades, early in the 20th century.

Left: "Aqua" and Crystal, 8"
   Hammer. $40-60.
Ruby and Crystal, 7 3/4"
   Hammer. $45-65.
Aqua and Crystal, 4 1/2"
   Hammer. $35-55.
Ruby and Crystal, 7 3/4"
   Hammer. $45-65.
Blue and Crystal, 6 1/2"
   Hatchet. $45-65.
      Attributed to Orie Mitchell.

Right: Detail of fake Tiffin label
on cane that reads 'Hand
Made Tiffin'.

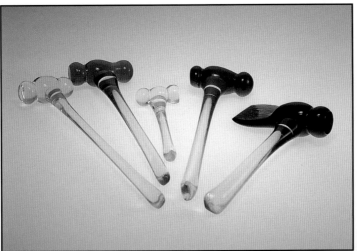

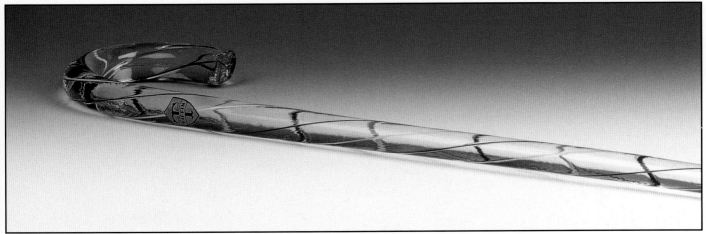

Sources

In addition to private archival documents, information for this book was taken from the following sources:

Bickenheuser, Fred. *Tiffin Glassmasters, Book I*. Grove City, Ohio: Glassmasters Publication, 1979.

_____. *Tiffin Glassmasters, Book II*. Grove City, Ohio: Glassmasters Publication, 1981.

_____. *Tiffin Glassmasters, Book III*. Grove City, Ohio: Glassmasters Publication, 1985.

O'Kane, Kelly, *Tiffin Glassmasters, the Modern Years*. St. Paul, Minnesota, 1998.

Goshe, Ed, et. al. *'40s, '50s & '60s Stemware by Tiffin*. Atglen, Pennsylvania: Schiffer Publishing, Ltd., 1999.

Jenks, Bill and Luna, Jerry. *Early American Pattern Glass 1850-1910*. Radnor, Pennsylvania: Wallace-Homestead Book Company, 1990.

Jenks, Bill, et. al. *Identifying Pattern Glass Reproductions*. Radnor, Pennsylvania: Wallace-Homestead Book Company, 1993.

Heacock, William and Bickenheuser, Fred. *Encyclopedia of Victorian Colored Pattern Glass, Book 5, U.S. Glass From A to Z*. Marietta, Ohio: Antique Publications, 1978.

Krause, Gail. *The Encyclopedia of Duncan Glass*. Tallahassee, Florida: Father and Son Associates, 1976.

Kovar, Lorraine. *Westmoreland Glass, 1950-1984*. Marietta, Ohio: Antique Publications, 1991.

China and Glass. Trade magazine. 1940s issues.

Crockery and Glass Journal. Trade magazine. 1940s issues.

United States Glass Company, catalogs and price listings: 1940, 1952, 1959-1962.

Duncan and Miller Division, catalog #93.

Tiffin Glass Company, catalogs and price listings, 1963-1979.

Tiffin Glass Collectors Club

The Tiffin Glass Collectors Club is a nonprofit corporation with tax exempt status, which was established in 1985 to study the history of Tiffin Glass (known as factory R) of the United States Glass Company, and the glassware manufactured there.

Membership in the club includes collectors from all over the United States. A club newsletter is published quarterly for members, and features minutes, glass articles, historical data and other information of interest to collectors.

Activities of the Tiffin Glass Collectors Club include the glass show held in June, and fund-raisers to benefit the Tiffin Glass Museum. The museum is located at 25 South Washington Street, in downtown Tiffin, Ohio.

For more information on the club or museum, inquiries may be directed to:

Tiffin Glass Collectors Club
P.O. Box 554
Tiffin, Ohio 44883

Index